ELEVATING CUSTOMER SERVICE IN HIGHER EDUCATION: A PRACTICAL GUIDE

HEATH BOICE-PARDEE
EMILY RICHARDSON
EILEEN SOISSON

ACADEMIC IMPRESSIONS | 2018
DENVER, CO

Published by Academic Impressions.

CR Mrig Company. 4601 DTC Blvd., Suite 800, Denver, CO 80237.

Copyright © 2018 Heath Boice-Pardee, Emily Richardson, and Eileen Soisson.

Cover design by Brady Stanton.

For reproduction, distribution, or copy permissions, or to order additional copies, please contact the Academic Impressions office at 720.488.6800 or visit:

http://bit.ly/2qbHuLr

Academic Impressions

ISBN: 978-1-948658-03-4

Printed in the United States of America.

CONTENTS

71 SECTION 4: SCRIPTING AND SERVICE EXCELLENCE

105 SECTION 5: CREATING ENVIRONMENTS THAT FACILITATE CUSTOMER SERVICE

124 SECTION 6: POLICIES AND PRACTICES THAT IMPACT SERVICE

146 SECTION 7: CULTIVATING FACULTY AND STAFF BUY-IN

INTRODUCTION

When Customer Service Meets Higher Education

Consider the following organizational values:

1. Creating a culture of warmth and belonging, where everyone is welcome.

2. Acting with courage, challenging the status quo.

3. Being present, connecting with transparency, dignity, and respect.

4. Our commitment to creativity, technology, and innovation generates unparalleled experiences that drive long-term value...

5. We do the right thing, all the time.

6. We care about the well-being and success of every person.

7. We make a difference in every community we serve.

8. We respect and listen to our people.

Since institutions of higher education are generally committed to enhancing diversity and community, providing for student success, and being places of education and caring, each of these core values could easily belong to a college or university; but this isn't the case. In fact, all of these statements come from companies known for providing exceptional customer service.

Exercise!

Which Organization's Values?

Look at the eight statements on the previous page. All eight came from one of these four companies recognized for its customer service: **Starbucks**, **Disney**, **Hilton**, and **Wegmans** supermarkets.

Try to guess which organization produced which statement—then check the answer key on page 7.

This fun exercise is also telling. Why are these the values of Disney or Starbucks—rather than the values of our local college or university? Once considered to be the ivory tower—revered and followed by society—academe has learned that it cannot rest on its historic or academic laurels any longer. In the changing landscape of higher education, colleges and universities increasingly have to compete to enroll and retain students who are "shopping" for better facilities, better services, better curricular and cocurricular opportunities, and better potential for getting a job (all at a reduced price).

It's in this context that colleges and universities are considering how to provide excellent service to students as customers. Yet there remains frequent resistance to considering college students as customers. The authors of this book contend that "students" and "customers" do not need to be mutually exclusive.

Perhaps the most pervasive argument against students as customers arises from how our colleagues understand a customer service concept from the early 1900s in London, when store owner Henry Gordon Selfridge adopted the philosophy, "the customer is always right." For over a century, this adage has been used widely, but there are many philosophical holes in this theory. We know that customers often need correcting; the customer *isn't* always right. Applying "the customer is always right" to students isn't appropriate or realistic in higher education, and we need to allay our colleagues' fears that this is what we mean by "customer service."

One way to understand what *do* we mean when we talk about providing students with improved customer service is to refer to our own experiences. As a customer, what do you expect and how do you like to be treated? The fact is that most customers don't expect to be right all the time; rather, they expect to be heard. As a customer, you probably have the following expectations—you expect providers to:

- Treat you with respect;

- Value your time;

- Listen to you;

- Apologize when things don't go as promised;

- Offer you the experience that was advertised;

- Care about your experience;

- Help you understand why specific decisions are made (whether you agree or not).

We contend that each of these is true of the expectations of most customers—*and* is true of students in higher education. There are many commonalities between "students" and "customers." By dispelling the illogical fear that if we treat students as customers they might demand specific grades, or feel entitled to a certain kind of conduct, we can hold a more thoughtful conversation about what it really means to approach students as customers.

A Roadmap for Using This Book

This book will be helpful to you whether or not you fully buy into the concept of students as customers. If your interest is to enhance student satisfaction, provide for a better student experience, improve retention, or make your office environment more conducive to getting work done, you will find many tips and tools to assist. This book also addresses other "customers" in higher education besides students—staff, faculty, parents, alumni, and community members, etc.

Each section will provide you with practical, hands-on exercises and/or worksheets to help you dig into your own customer service challenges in higher education. Throughout the book, you will see worksheets and exercises to help you investigate issues more deeply. Watch for:

Consider This... **Exercise!** **Fun Fact!**

The book consists of 8 sections:

Section 1: Learning from Service Industry Leaders

This section will provide insight into industry leaders known for providing excellent customer service including Marriott and Hilton, Starbucks, Disney, Universal, and more. Specific research and examples, including the customer service philosophy behind each model, will be outlined for application in higher education settings.

Section 2: Developing Service Competencies

This section will provide a roadmap for identifying the service competencies needed to provide excellent customer service in higher education based on general and specific functional areas.

Section 3: How to Support Frontline Staff in Enhancing Customer Service

This section will discuss frontline staff and their specific role in providing high-level customer service. Strategies for coaching and supporting frontline staff, as well as insight into ways to manage stress, will be covered.

Section 4: Scripting and Service Excellence

This section will discuss the benefits of "scripting" in higher education. Phone greetings, responses to regular questions, and ways to manage complaints will be highlighted. Training staff and students on the use of scripts will also be covered.

Section 5: Creating Environments that Facilitate Customer Service

This section will cover the creation of physical environments that facilitate positive interactions with customers in higher education.

Section 6: Policies and Practices that Impact Customer Service

This section will discuss the myriad of policies and practices used in higher education and their impact on customer satisfaction. Gaining an understanding of federal, state, institutional, and office-specific policies and practices will be discussed and reviewed. Specific focus on developing institutional policies and practices that enhance customer service will be reviewed.

Section 7: Cultivating Faculty and Staff Buy-In

This section will discuss how some campus partners may not immediately buy into the concept of enhancing customer service in the higher education setting and outline strategies to increase participation.

Section 8: Post-Secondary Examples of Customer Service Excellence

This section will discuss specific examples of colleges and universities who are implementing policies, practices, and philosophies to enhance customer service on-campus. Examples of institutions who are known for providing excellent customer service, as well as schools who are new to implementing new strategies, will be discussed.

We hope that the material in this book will capture your interest in improving experiences for your customers, challenge you and your team, and facilitate your own creativity. If you have questions or comments for the authors, or for Academic Impressions, please reach out to us. After all, you are the customer and while you may not always be right, you deserve to be heard.

GET CERTIFIED AS A CUSTOMER SERVICE PRO

Become a customer service expert by attending one of Academic Impressions' certification trainings. These events provide in-depth instruction with top customer service experts in higher education, and allow plenty of time for role-playing and practicing the core skills of good customer service. The conference culminates in a final written exam and you will receive a certificate of completion for your time spent and knowledge gained at this event. Show that your campus is a leader in customer service: get your entire front-line staff certified! We also provide on-campus certification workshops.

Interested? Contact Amit Mrig, President, Academic Impressions:

amit@academicimpressions.com

(KEY: 1-3, Starbucks; 4, Disney; 5, Hilton; 6-8, Wegmans)

SECTION 1: LEARNING FROM SERVICE INDUSTRY LEADERS

Lead author for this chapter: Emily Richardson.

So where does one begin with creating a customer service philosophy for their department, school, or university? A focus on customer service may be newer to higher education, but because it isn't new everywhere. One place to look is at examples of excellence outside of the higher education sector, in business and industry. The concept of service has changed dramatically with the advent of Internet retailers, but even web-based retail models have made a conscious decision about their philosophy to enable them to meet the customer's needs. We are also seeing an additional change, one that focuses on self-service and only requires human intervention when the situation can't be handled through basic self-service. So when did service become so important to everything that we do?

In 1982, Tom Peters and Robert H. Waterman, Jr. wrote a book called *In Search of Excellence*, which catalogued the business practices behind successful companies. One of the key factors listed in the book was "close to the customer," and they used the phrase to describe such companies as Disney, Marriott Hotels, and Neiman Marcus. One statement that rings true for higher education that should be considered when thinking about service is: "a simple summary of what our research uncovered on the customer attribute is this: the excellent companies really are close to their customers. That's it. Other companies talk about it; the excellent companies do it" (p. 156).

This book was followed three years later by a book titled *Service America! Doing Business in the New Economy*, written by Ron Zemke and Karl Albrecht. In the book, Zemke and Albrecht declared that the current economy was actually the service economy. They talked about the importance of managing the service encounter by designing a service system and hiring the right people. These books led the way for retailers, hotels, and businesses thinking about customer service more seriously for the first time. There was a realization that those who were working hard at giving their customers superior service were producing the best results.

This also led to an entire group of books focused on what a company needs to do to serve customers well and to get the customer to return. This is a simple statement, but one that is powerful: a restaurant or a hotel wants a repeat customer, because repeat business is less expensive than advertising to find a new customer. In higher education, it is the same thing: we want a student to return the next semester, an alumni to return to campus or to provide a donation, a conference participant to recommend the school to their child, an attendee at a sporting event, or a musical performance to return again to the campus. While higher education is unique in many ways, in this respect we are the same as any other business: we want and need our customers to return again.

The Research on Customer Service

At the same time that Peters and Waterman were writing their books, Jan Carlzon became the president of Scandinavian Airlines, which was having financial trouble.

He adopted the concept of a moment of truth, which he described as follows in his book *Moments of Truth*:

"Anytime a customer comes into contact with any aspect of a business, however remote, is an opportunity to form an impression."

The idea was that every employee, regardless of their job or title, had an opportunity to make an impression on a customer.

To illustrate this concept, let me share an example of a "moment of truth" from my own experience. Preparing for a recent trip to a conference, my administrative assistant accidentally made a mistake with the flight reservation. The day before the trip, I had no way to check in online because the name on my driver's license did not match the name on the ticket. The name on the ticket was that of my administrative assistant!

The phone call to the airline yielded an hour wait time, so—living close to the local airport—the airline's ticketing desk became the next logical stop. The phone call to the airline yielded an hour wait time, so—living close to the local airport—that became the next stop. The wait in line for a ticket agent went quickly, but I wasn't anticipating a great result. I knew the mistake had been made and that typically airlines will charge for reservation changes, so I fully expected to walk away saddled with fees.

When I reached the counter, though, the result blew me away. The agent listened, empathized, and then explained that although the current ticket would not be valid, they could issue a voucher for future travel to my administrative assistant. This was great for her, but it still didn't solve my need for travel for the next day to speak at a conference. The agent continued to listen, and then proceeded to issue a new ticket. Not only was it a new ticket, but it was issued at the same rate used for the original ticket, and—by way of apology for the experience I had had on the phone—they also upgraded the ticket and provided me with access to the airport lounge! Through that interaction, the employee made me a lifetime customer. This was what Carlzon described as a moment of truth.

Take a moment to think about this in the context of your own life. Have you had an experience, say, in a restaurant where the host or hostess sat you on time and the server was superb, but then the wine sommelier treated you poorly when you asked the difference between a Merlot from Argentina and one from Australia? Each individual in this story makes up the full service experience, and everyone has a chance to make their own impression with you as the customer.

In 1993, Ken Blanchard (the author of *The One Minute Manager*) co-authored with Sheldon Bowles a book titled *Raving Fans, A Revolutionary Approach to Customer Service.* This book features the tale of a man named Charlie, who helps a manager determine the three secrets for developing customers into "raving fans." The first key is to **Decide what you want** by creating a vision of perfection centered on the customer.

Do you have a vision for customer service at your institution of higher education? Can you paint that picture for others? A service strategy is a distinctive formula for delivering service that is valuable for the customer. Disney's is simple: "To make people happy." You might find hints in the mission or vision statement for your institution as to the expectations for students. But remember that customers can be parents, alumni, coworkers, conference attendees, AND prospective students to name just a few. A customer service strategy must be applicable to all.

Exercise!

Create a Vision Board

What is your vision for what your customers should experience? A vision board may help you and your team establish ideas. Print photos or phrases from the Internet, or cut pictures and words from magazines that represent what you want to offer your customers. Paste these to a poster board and hang it in the office for quick reminders and encouragement!

Charlie, the main character in Blanchard and Bowles' book, then explains that you need to **Discover what the customer wants.** You can better understand what the customer wants if you first have your own vision. Then, the customer's vision will help you fill in the gaps and determine what to ignore. One idea to help you discover what your customers want would be to hold a focus group comprised of different types of customers and ask them what they think about your vision statement—what is missing and what is important. Your work group might think, for example, that communicating weekly to your student population is enough to keep them apprised of activities happening on campus, but you might learn from your focus group that in fact bi-weekly communication would be better due to the sheer number of emails they receive.

The third secret is to **Deliver plus one.** This secret is about developing the consistency that must be present every time a customer experiences service within your organization. There is no question that consistency of service within any specific office can make a difference. Recently at my own institution, it was requested that a department on campus continue to serve students in the same way that they always had—yet their department had been reorganized, and half of the employees had been moved to a new location with different duties. The expectation for maintaining consistency in this case was impossible due to the work obligations of those left within the department. **Deliver plus one** was not the standard, and all consistency was lost. Providing consistent service must be a key component in all staffing decisions, and yet it is often not considered during times of change.

Consider This...

Read *Raving Fans*

Consider reading Ken Blanchard and Sheldon Bowles' book together, as a department. Then hold a brown bag lunch to discuss the book, and have team members discuss how this book applies to your department.

There is another book I recommend—*Fabled Service, Ordinary Acts, Extraordinary Outcomes*—that was written by Betsy Sanders in 1995. It is a story about how a company can reach what they call "fabled service," and it features retailer Nordstrom as the primary example. But what actually *is* fabled service? The book defines it as such: "Service only becomes significant (fabled) when it is so meaningful to your customers that they articulate and proclaim it."

Think about this statement personally. When was the last time you received such excellent service that you raved about it to your friends and neighbors? The extraordinary service you received was so great, that you are willing to tell others about your experience.

Star ratings in the online world have become the way an individual "proclaims" their impression about a product. Amazon often sends requests for an individual to rank the packaging or delivery from a vendor they use. After a trip, Travelocity will ask you to rate your experience through the use of stars. *Fabled Service* was written before the Internet explosion, yet the ability to tell others about service has become even more accessible with your iPhone or Android device.

To achieve Fabled Service, the book recommends that you think more broadly about service in general:

- Think as your customer thinks; the customer defines fabled service.

- Realize that service is everything your company does, and thus becomes everyone's job.

- Integrate service into everything you do.

- Service is a cost of doing business, and you need to design the system right.

- Service can and will impact revenues.

- Focus on the growth of those in your company who serve others.

In 2004 we saw *The Fred Factor* by Mark Sandborn reach the best seller list. In 2013, Sanborn published *Fred 2.0: New Ideas on How to keep delivering Extraordinary Results*, and once again we learned more about Fred, his postman, who consistently delivered service in simple yet remarkable ways. Can you imagine getting flowers on Mother's day from your postman? This is not a book about normal or average workers. Instead, this is a book about those individuals who are choosing to be extraordinary in the way they treat those whom they serve. Think about this quote from Fred: "I like doing things for people because it makes me feel better. I know I've done a good job if I take care of my customers—although I don't think of them as customers; I think of them as my friends or the folks on my route. Some people may not even have a clue what I've done for them, but that's okay. I don't do it so they'll know—I do it because it's the right thing to do."

Can you think of individuals at your university who are just average? Most of us certainly can. By contrast, it is much harder to think of those who are extraordinary all the time. Yet for us to achieve excellence in customer service, we need individuals who are committed to working with passion and to providing the best service possible to every employee.

The Recent Growth of a Service Focus in Higher Education

The book *Embrace the Oxymoron: Customer Service in Higher Education* by Dr. Neal Raisman paints a bigger picture of customer service in higher education. "Colleges are starting to see higher education in business-like realities. They are realizing that revenue depends on selling the college (recruitment) to its customers (students and parents). Sales (enrollment) are made based on the college's brand (image), product (courses, programs, degrees), and by creating a connection with the customer (customer service)."

In light of the current economy, political climate, and widespread competition, many universities are seeing decreases in revenue, lower retention rates, and universal cutbacks. In response, service excellence within higher education has become an idea that more administrators are welcoming on their campuses.

Five years ago, there were approximately 10 higher education institutions providing a university-wide customer service program. Those institutions were mostly in the state of Georgia because of a governor mandate that any state monies for education must have some sort of service focus. In 2017, we have been able to identify at least 118 institutions with a program specifically focused on customer service within higher education.

As much as some people in colleges and universities may still cringe at the term "customer service," colleges and universities are businesses at their core and must address the reality of customer service in higher education settings. The reality of increased competition in higher education, the rising expectations of customers, and the challenge of retention are three main reasons why we are seeing unprecedented growth in the number of customer service programs in higher education.

Increased Competition in Higher Education

The increased competition in higher education contributes to the need for better service and a more student-focused experience. Universities and colleges are much more competitive due to the new options available for learning. In the 1990s, an online college degree was not an option, let alone an online college class; whereas, today many such programs exist. Thanks to the ease of transportation and modern technology, students today are more able and willing to travel to an out-of-state school than they were decades ago. Today, there are also a variety of avenues by which students can achieve a college degree and define the experience. There are more schools to attend, to transfer into, and from which to graduate.

Years ago, the idea of free education was laughable. In April 2017, New York lawmakers approved a scholarship proposed by Governor Andrew Cuomo that would be available to individuals whose families earn $125,000 or less annually. The scholarship would cover all tuition for two- and four-year public colleges. While other states may offer free community college, New York is the first to make free tuition available at four-year public colleges, and there is sure to be a ripple effect to colleges competing for that same student.

Rising Expectations of Our Customers

Students and their families have greater exposure than ever to the available options provided by different colleges, and with that exposure comes higher expectations. They can compare and contrast with a standard of what they are looking for in and throughout the college experience. If one school rolls out the red carpet for incoming students (e.g., provides a luncheon with an opportunity to meet future faculty and staff), while another school only sends a form letter, students who experience the latter may respond with disappointment. This is especially the case if the incoming student's family or friends have experienced the other, more personal level of service instead.

Customers will have basic expectations when it comes to service and how they want to be treated. Boyd (2012) shares specific tips that academic advisers and other institutional officials can follow to provide quality service when interacting with a student, and these are applicable to the expectations of any customer:

- Treat students with dignity and respect. This is a basic human necessity and right.

- Give students clear directions on how to solve their problems and issues. Students should not be given the runaround. Students are at college to study and learn, not go on a wild goose chase all over campus trying to find the answers to simple questions.

- Be responsive to students and their parents. "If you tell a parent you will call them back today, then call them back today" (Ewers, p. 2). Being true to your word means a lot to students and their families.

- Provide timely answers to students' questions and give regular feedback on their progress.

These tips are specific to individual service interactions, but it is even better if an institution as a whole takes the time to identify and learn about the expectations of its various customers. Based on that student's background or story, what one customer expects may be very different from what another would expect.

The Challenge of Retention

The concept of "if you treat them well, they will stay" seems to make a service program seem very simplistic. But there is in fact some truth to that concept.

Why do students leave college? Does service have anything to do with students transferring to another school?

Dr. Neal Raisman's research shows that 44 percent of students nationwide leave a university due to the perception that they were treated poorly or that the college didn't care about them. This research is shared in the chart on the next page, and such information about retention is the foundation for Coastal Carolina University's service initiative. Coastal Carolina University (CCU) launched a service excellence initiative in 2012 called Feel the Teal®. (You can read more about the initiative in Section 8 of this book.) CCU's university-wide customer service plan is designed to improve service delivery and increase customer satisfaction and retention. Raisman's research is shared with all new employees to stress the importance of service excellence and how it ties to retention.

According to Raisman's study:

Twenty-four percent of college students will leave because of the perception that they were treated poorly or received bad service.

Students are consumer-oriented. They see themselves as customers who should be treated well, especially as the cost of attending college continues to rise. Students clearly relate the amount they are paying to the way they believe and feel they should be treated and served. Participants in the study did not necessarily link paying tuition to a sense of privilege, but they did indicate that they expect high-quality service in exchange for the amount of money they were paying. One student elaborated on this perspective in the study: "I am paying a lot of money and I don't care that she said they were understaffed. For what I am paying, they should have more staff and better service."

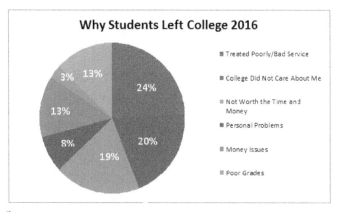

Source:
http://academicmaps.blogspot.com/2016/09/why-students-left-college-2016-neal.html

Many students cited that they had trouble getting help when they needed it, described "sour-faced clerks hassling them," and reported being sent from office to office in search of a solution. All too often, their problem or issue remained unresolved, even after "the shuffle." Students stated that they were often unable to find a satisfactory solution or even proper attention to their request for assistance.

> **Twenty percent of students will leave due to the perception the college/university doesn't care about them.**

In this scenario, students are made to feel like a number and because of that, it is easier for them to leave. This is an important statistic since it clearly points to a lack of engagement on the part of colleges with these students. This data is a useful reminder that everyone has a natural need to feel valued and welcomed if they are to engage back. We must find ways to build connectedness with students through person-to-person engagement that extends beyond social media. If a student perceives that he or she is not cared about or does not belong, that student will be much more likely to drop out and seek another person, group, or college that values and welcomes him or her in a more meaningful way.

A common statement made by students in the study was "all they cared about was my money but after that they paid me no attention." This indicates that colleges are not engaging students as well as is necessary to keep them. Schools need to maintain positive contact with students and engage them with some activity or aspect of the college. The Citadel and other military schools create engagement through shared experiences and a pride in the school's corps. Engagement makes students feel closer to the school, and thus a part of it, and that helps to overcome the feeling that they are attending a faceless institution that does not care for or about them.

Nineteen percent of students will leave because they believe that what they are going through does not have value and is not worth it.

This is related to the cost and service issues of the most common response, as discussed above. Students are coming to campus with a very strong return on investment proposition. College is supposed to lead to a job and a career: students go to college to get the education and training they need to get hired. However, they are hearing from the media that many students who graduate from college today are not getting jobs, or are working in areas not related to their area of study. This causes them to be wary about the amount of money and time they are putting in, so—more than ever—they are demanding a clear return on their investment.

Regarding the benefits of good customer-student relationships, Emery, et al., said, "Student-customer satisfaction directly correlates to larger enrollments: Happy students stay in school, so retention rates remain high; happy students tell their high-school friends, so recruitment numbers are higher..." (p. 2). More students generate more tuition revenue, and in the current economic reality, this tells us that service excellence must be threaded throughout higher education operations and practices.

For colleges and universities that place a vision and value on service excellence, rewards can translate into increased revenue through improved recruitment and retention, reduced recruitment costs, improved service and satisfaction, quicker yield conversions, and closer internal working relationships. This term of "customer service" is still new and somewhat foreign in higher education, but it is sure to give the institutions that embrace it a competitive advantage in the future. To seize that advantage, it's important to see what lessons we can learn from successful high-service organizations in other industries that have a long track record of providing excellent service.

Examples from High-Service Organizations Today

It is one thing to talk about customer service theory, but quite another to see it in action. There are multiple other organizations for us to consider and learn from. They include hotels, resorts, restaurants, grocery stores, and other online retailers. Each one recognized here has service to the customer as a key to their vision and strategy.

Delivering WOW service has been made famous by Zappos, since WOW is their #1 core value. Their mission has been aligned around the concept of providing the best customer service possible. This means going above and beyond to please customers, co-workers, vendors, and partners.

When Zappos began to sell shoes in 1999, the prevailing wisdom was that the customer will buy from "the company with the best service and the best selection." As an online vendor, Zappos realized that to stand out from their competition they needed to not only ensure selection, but also empower their employees to provide higher-quality and higher-speed service. To understand the Zappos model of service, take a few minutes to visit the customer testimonials page on their website. Their WOW service is attested throughout the customer comments, where you will see superlatives like "amazing," "the best," "awesome," and "excellence."

Consider This...

What customer communications do you receive?

Think about the letters you have received from customers. What types of words are they using? Do they comment using words similar to the "WOW" at Zappos?

Or are they letters of complaint, telling you how their service expectations were not met? Which kind of letter would you rather receive?

When I think about excellence in customer service, Disney happens to be at the top of my list. As previously stated, their vision is "To Make People Happy," and if you have ever visited their operation, you have seen that they do everything possible to make that happen. Having students who worked for Disney, I got the opportunity to spend time with their casting department (Human Resources) to learn about how they hire and train employees. The original video from *In Search of Excellence* consisted of a 15 minute segment about the hiring process at Disney and the way they make sure that employees are trained and prepared for customer service. Here are just a few things that they do:

- They know that people coming into the parks first thing in the morning are excited about the opportunities that await them. They also know that at the end of the day, guests are tired and just want to get to their cars. So they deliberately hire to ensure that upbeat, energetic individuals are able to work the morning shift, while quieter (but direction focused) individuals help people out of the park and to the parking and transportation areas.

- The individuals who clean the park during the day are taught that the most familiar phrase they will hear is "Where are the bathrooms?" They are taught to answer that with a fresh eye, because even though they may have heard the question a dozen times already, each person asking is a brand new customer.

- The Disney characters are taught to realize that those in wheelchairs won't have the same access to them. Instead of waiting for these guests to come to them, the characters approach these guests, so they too can experience the wonder of Disney.

A hotel chain that must be mentioned when discussing service excellence is Ritz Carlton, which in 1983 became The Ritz Carlton Hotel Company LLC. As they grew in number, they also grew in service excellence, especially during the time when Horse Schulze was CEO of the company. During his leadership, they became known for the motto "We are Ladies and Gentleman serving Ladies and Gentlemen," and they used this concept to empower their employees. They trained front line staff to accommodate the needs of their guests (within reason) without having to go to a supervisor to gain approval. Still today, their "Gold Standards" include multiple references to serving their guests, and they encourage their employees to offer sincere greetings, to use guests' names, to offer fond farewells, and to own and solve guest problems. The Ritz Carlton won the Malcolm Baldrige National Quality Award in 1992. In 1998, Marriott purchased the chain.

During my academic year in hospitality management, I was able to attend a conference on Quality Management where Horse Schulze spoke to academic and hospitality managers about their efforts to meet and exceed guest expectations. The concept of customer first as a value proposition was the piece that continues to remain front and center in my memory today. He spoke of his employees as the key to whether or not the company would succeed and the care that must be given for the employees to buy into the vision and the dream of customer service. Each employee carried a lamented card in their pocket that had the company's motto and vision imprinted, as a daily reminder to the employee that they were part of something larger.

There is also no shortage of restaurants that have the customer first in their mind, but Starbucks rises to the top as one that has designed their operations and trained their employees the best in relation to customer service excellence. In their booklet for their employees, "Business Ethics and Compliance," the following is stated: "We are all caretakers of the Starbucks reputation. How we conduct our business and how we treat others—our fellow partners, customers, communities, suppliers and share-holders—will continue to determine how the world views Starbucks." This statement immediately puts forth the importance of customers, but also speaks to how they are to be treated: There is the expectation of excellence in service. The booklet continues on page 10 to talk about how they want customers to be treated: "Legendary customer service is a top priority at Starbucks. We strive to make every customer's experience pleasant and fulfilling, and we treat our customers as we treat one another, with respect and dignity. This means, for example, that we never harass or discriminate against our customers."

One cannot go into a Starbucks and expect anything different when this type of information is available online. Their stores have become the neighborhood hangout, where friends go to meet, where business occurs, and where individuals take a moment to relax with a great cup of coffee. Once again, this is made possible by their emphasis on customer service and the expectations they set for how their employees should treat the customer.

What examples can you think of?

Use regional examples when talking about customer service to your colleagues or employees. They will relate to the companies they know and can start to make comparisons with the service they're providing.

Consider This...

From Worst-Case to Defining Moment

We offered a brief sampling of how Disney makes service count throughout their hotels, restaurants, and theme parks. None of their employees are average—they are all expected to be extraordinary. As a guest of Disney many years ago with three young boys, I got to experience Disney service excellence in a surprising way. Within two hours of checking into our cabin at Camp Wilderness, I slipped and broke my ankle, and my husband had to call for help to get me to a hospital. That in itself was well done, but it was the service after we returned to the cabin that blew me away. The service concierge came to meet with us and assured us that we should stay and see the parks. Given crutches at the hospital, I couldn't imagine getting around the park. Suddenly there was a wheelchair at my disposal, and they ordered a wheelchair accessible bus to follow the route we would take so that I could easily get in and out of the parks. Once in the parks, we also realized that there were special entrances for those in wheelchairs. For four days, each and every day, the service concierge called and connected with us to ensure that we had what we needed during our stay, and they continually delivered excellence in service. The best part of it all was having front row seats for the parades. The experience showed me how proper planning and training on an organization's part can make the best out of an unforeseeable situation on the customer's part.

I have a degree in the hospitality industry, and I worked in restaurants, resorts and hotels for many years before changing over to higher education. I'd like to share one of my customer service experiences in that vein to demonstrate what you can do, even under the most difficult conditions, to make customers content and happy.

I had the privilege to work in Maui, Hawaii at a luxury resort that was known for beautiful views, exquisite furnishings and excellence in food service. As the food service manager, I had responsibility for a 250 seat dining room that filled every evening. It was designed in a Hawaiian theme, with plantings, statuettes, and lighting that set the mood for this indoor/outdoor restaurant overlooking the ocean. One evening, the restaurant was fully booked and busy. At about 8:00 p.m., the sprinklers that were embedded in the beds of flowers and plants proceeded to go off with full pressure, getting every guest—yes, all 250 of them—soaking wet, along with their food, clothes, the tablecloths, and the tile floors. Oh yes, and the servers, including myself, were also very wet. It was an occasion when I didn't know whether I should laugh or cry, but I knew neither of those responses were going to be appropriate. Instead, we moved rapidly into action, calling for every employee from the hotel to come to the dining room. We secured every pool towel from the pool and handed them out to guests. At the same time, we had our bartenders walk around to the tables and mix drinks for guests, and had our chefs begin the process of making brand new dishes for those that requested them.

In the end, we did have to write off some of the charges and offer vouchers for another meal, but it was the hard work by the entire staff that did not go unnoticed by the customers. They realized that the problem wasn't ours, but that with extraordinary hard work, we were going to make things right for them. Instead of closing at 9:30 p.m., we were still serving at midnight. At about 12:30 a.m., one couple who had just been seated at 8:00 p.m. when the sprinklers first went off were leaving the dining room, and they hunted me down. The gentleman commended my staff for their hard work in making sure they still had a wonderful evening, and then handed me $500.00 to split amongst the staff present. He asked to hear our secret for hiring people who were extraordinary in their work ethic. I had not thought about that element before, but it was true: we were able to find workers who really cared about the customers and went out of their way to make them happy. All I could offer was that I was privileged to have found them, but I truly couldn't answer "how" we had done so. It wasn't until I started to study the theories and concepts in the books that came out in the years after this experience that I realized I had been hiring for the passion to serve, not for ability or knowledge about service. Abilities and knowledge can be learned, but passion cannot be taught.

Final Thoughts

So what can we learn that we can use in higher education regarding customer service? First, it is all about the people we hire and how we prepare them for their work with all of our customers. We need to make sure that there is a clear vision regarding our service strategy, and make sure they know what is important and necessary to be done consistently to ensure lasting excellence in customer service. We need to consider our staging, design, and operations in terms of how the customer will use them to achieve service, as well as what policies might be in place that don't allow us to offer the service that we should. Finally, we need to realize that customer service isn't a new thing. Instead, it is one that can and should be translated into the world of higher education, and become one additional way that we can differentiate value in our institutions.

Finally, as a leader in higher education, you need to keep the context defined in this chapter in mind as you read in the chapters that follow about service competencies— whether for frontline staff, faculty, or administrators. These competencies (coupled with policies, processes, and an environment built with the customer in mind) will begin to change the culture to one that is centered on "customer first," moments of truth, and a focus on quality service at your institution.

SECTION 2: DEVELOPING SERVICE COMPETENCIES

Lead author for this chapter: Heath Boice-Pardee.

What do you value in your organization? What do your customers value from your organization when it comes to service delivery? These questions will assist you in identifying what is important for the development of service competencies.

Exercise!

Take a moment alone or with your team to consider the following:

- Who are your customers?

- What do your customers need?

- What do you need?

- What commonalities/intersections exist?

Who Are Your Customers?

The Big Sandwich or the Super Deluxe Sandwich?

In order to determine what service competencies your customers value most, you will first have to identify who your customers are. To illustrate service competencies, consider your local fast-food restaurant. As a customer, what do you value when you visit? You probably want the person taking your order to know about the products, right? They should be able to explain to you the difference between the Big Sandwich and the Super Deluxe Sandwich, which will likely impact your buying choice. So, "content knowledge" is a service competency that is important to you. Likewise, you probably want the person behind the counter to not only answer your questions, but to be polite and helpful. In this regard, "interpersonal skills" are surely another service competency that is important to you.

Given this example, who are your customers? Here's what we know. They are people who eat fast food. They value service providers with specific content knowledge and strong interpersonal skills. But that's about all. Although we can make assumptions about other characteristics on the basis that they entered the fast food restaurant, we shouldn't. Does eating fast food mean that they aren't fit and don't care about their health? Does eating fast food mean that they are on a tight budget or simply frugal? Once you identify who your customers are, you may then begin to identify what they need. This will help you further understand what service competencies are important to them.

What Do Your Customers Need?

To develop service competencies for your organization, you must identify what your customers need. While this question may seem overwhelming, you likely already have the answers. Start with the basics and then add specifics. For example, you may easily identify that your customers (e.g., students, staff, faculty, etc.) need:

- Reliability

- Clear messages

- Conducive environments

- Patience

- Care

The next step is identifying how to provide these. For example:

- **Reliability:** Is your front desk consistently staffed? Are your hours of service posted prominently?

- **Clear messages:** Do you train anyone who answers the phone/email how to respond? Do you use a script?

- **Conducive environments:** Are your physical spaces welcoming? Do customers feel comfortable approaching front line staff?

- **Patience:** Have you devised ways to let staff get away from their desk to decompress? Have you shared your expectations for dealing with challenging customers?

- **Care:** Do you role model how to show care for customers? Have you shared your expectations with your staff?

SAMPLE CUSTOMER QUESTIONNAIRE

You need to understand what is important to your customers. Ask for feedback personally or via a brief survey. Here is a sample questionnaire; tailor these ten questions to your unique customers and to the needs of your department.

1. Accuracy of information is more important than how fast I get an answer or response.

    1   2   3   4   5

Disagree   Agree

2. I would prefer to get information:

    A.   In person
    B.   Via email
    C.   Via text
    D.   Via phone

3. A personal connection with an office is important to me:

    1   2   3   4   5

Disagree   Agree

SAMPLE CUSTOMER QUESTIONNAIRE, CONTINUED

4. I would prefer the following hours of service (please check all that apply):*

A. Early morning before 8:30 a.m.
B. 8:30 a.m. to 4:30 p.m.
    (typical business hours)
C. 4:30 p.m. to 7:30 p.m.

> * Remember, don't offer a choice that you're not prepared to offer.

5. When I email an office, I prefer to get a response within:

A. 1 hour
B. 2-4 hours
C. Within the same business day
D. Within 24 hours
E. Within a week

6. What is one program or service that we don't currently provide that you wish we would?

7. Was there a time when our department didn't meet your expectations? We'd like to hear about that experience:

8. How likely would you recommend our department/program/services to other students?

     A.   Very Likely
     B.   Likely
     C.   Neutral
     D.   Not Likely
     E.   Never

9. How did you hear about our department/ program/service (check all that apply)?

     A.   Word of mouth
     B.   Poster/flyer
     C.   Email
     D.   Social media post (Twitter, Facebook, etc.)
     E.   Website
     F.   Other (please describe):

10. What else would you like us to know?

Identifying Service Competencies

When considering what service competencies are important to your organization, it's important to start broad and then get more specific. Think of the broad core competencies as umbrella categories and the more specific as "job-specific" categories. For example, one of your organization's core competencies might be "Multicultural Competence." Under that broad umbrella, you should identify corresponding job-specific competencies which may vary greatly from department to department. For example, a department who serves international students may require staff to possess specific knowledge of immigration law in order to be considered "Multiculturally Competent"; however, in another department, being sensitive to the needs of LGBTQ students may meet the criteria for the category.

Keeping Customers in Mind

When identifying service competencies, a good place to begin is with your customers. As stated previously, it is essential that you identify who your customers are. In higher education, your customers are likely students, faculty, staff, alumni, parents, community members, and others. It will be easiest for staff to implement specific service competencies if they are shared among all customer constituencies. For example, the competencies created to serve students (content knowledge, for example) are the same as the competencies used with parents and alumni (who are also looking for content knowledge).

So how should you begin to identify which service competencies are necessary for your organization? First, ask: What do your customers need? There are a few ways to approach this question, including:

1. **Ask them.** If you're not sure what your customers need or expect when it comes to receiving great service, don't leave it to chance. If you aren't sure, ask them. This can be accomplished through the development of a brief survey (written or electronic) that your customers complete. Don't worry about collecting hundreds of surveys, even 20-30 will give you the "pulse" of what your customers are looking for.

2. **Consider the questions.** What are the most commonly asked questions for your department? Reflecting on these will give you valuable insight into what your customers need. For example, if the person staffing your reception area is constantly asked the same questions repeatedly, such as, "How do I submit my timecard?," patience is likely a necessary service competency.

3. **Look for issues.** Sometimes a service competency needs to be met with a change to physical environment. For example, do you ever receive feedback that your staff doesn't seem approachable? Look for the reasons, even physical barriers, to providing service. Are customers greeted by staff who have their backs facing them? Are there barriers, glass panels, or other obstructions to service interactions? If so, you might consider changing the physical environment to facilitate great service delivery!

Fun Fact!

It is commonly stated that the Number One question asked at Walt Disney World is, "What time is the three o'clock parade?" Through research, Disney determined that guests *do* know what time the parade begins, and that ascertaining the correct time is not the real meaning of their question. What guests really want to know is when they should begin lining up, where they should stand for a better view, and how long the parade lasts. Be sure to always dig deeper to uncover the real meaning behind customers' questions!

One good idea is to **keep an FAQ log**—you can see a sample on the next page. This worksheet can help you identify the frequently asked questions (FAQs) that your frontline staff need to have immediate answers for, and that should be posted on your website. Keeping an FAQ log will also help you identify what questions you *don't* have answers to yet—where there are some trouble spots!

SAMPLE FAQ LOG

Keep a copy of this Frequently Asked Questions log at your front desk, reception area, and with any staff who answer questions for your department.

You may find it useful to document the responses given to frequent questions in order to compare notes for accuracy. In some cases, you may find that some staff use language that you'll want to use department-wide. Be sure to compare logs regularly and update your FAQs at reception areas, manuals, and online!

Question you received:

How you responded:

Other questions they likely have but didn't think to ask:

If there is room for improvement in our response, what more helpful answer should we give next time?

What Do You Need?

As a frontline staff member or manager you may have many thoughts on necessary service competencies that will help ease your work flow and increase office efficiency, but keep in mind, this isn't about you. Your needs should be secondary to the needs of the customer. For example, as a manager, you may need to have your frontline staff take a lunch from 12:00 p.m. to 1:00 p.m. in order for them to meet labor standards and allow them to eat lunch together. This allows you to ensure that your staff are taking lunch and also allows you to plan for lunch breaks out of the office. Your customers, however, may say that getting business done during lunch is the best time for them. So, while the normal lunch hour may work best for you in terms of scheduling and accounting, it may not work for your customers.

The same can be said for office hours. While standard office hours at your university might be 8:30 p.m. to 4:30 p.m., do these hours meet your customers' needs? How many students come in and out of your doors before 10:00 a.m.? Likewise, would office traffic increase if you stayed open until 6:00 p.m. or later? Modifying office hours may not only enhance customer satisfaction but also offer your staff some flexibility their work schedules. It is possible to meet your needs in managing your office while also meeting, or exceeding, your customer's expectations. Just remember, customer service in your department should not be only about you!

What Intersections Exist?

Even though customer service isn't about you, your needs do matter in order to get business done. After all, you know how to manage your area best. It's rare that there aren't intersections between the needs of the customer and your needs. Look for these commonalities in order to enhance overall satisfaction.

For example, if you cannot find the necessary resources to extend or shift office hours, how might you expand your online presence? Boosting information and "self-services" online will allow you to extend your department's reach 24 hours a day, while also maintaining routine office operations your staff might enjoy. I have worked at a university that used to require all student employees to physically go to the student employment office on-campus to complete required hiring paperwork. Typically, this is fine for most students; however, since some students are able to work remotely and may not be on-campus every day, this requirement is not customer-centric. I suggested that the office allow students to complete this paperwork from wherever they are, making sure that all legal documents are signed and verified in the presence of a notary public (which is the same as the process used for non-student employees). Although hesitant at first, the office has implemented this practice which is more student-friendly and allows staff to meet necessary legal requirements.

Case Study

Like many learning experiences, the best way to understand something is to consider its practical application. At one institution where I worked, we had an opportunity to change the "Information Desk" in the student union to a "Welcome Center" (See Section 6 of this book for details). In order to assess the service competencies necessary for this, we considered what wasn't working in the "Information Desk." A quick environmental scan showed that the existing enterprise was lacking in the following areas:

- **Physical Space:** The information desk was a dark space tucked away in the building.

- **Interpersonal Access:** The existing information desk had a computer for attendants to use, but it was recessed into the desk so when customers approached, they only saw the tops of the attendants' heads. This didn't enhance interpersonal communication.

We determined that if we could modify this area to mitigate these issues, we could enhance service to anyone who sought information. In terms of service competencies, we knew we needed to make some changes, including:

- Providing better access to customers;

- Modifying physical space to enhance customer interaction;

- Enhancing training for attendants to communicate with customers;

- Creating an attendant uniform to enhance professionalism and customer confidence.

Understanding these needs allowed us to refine the service competencies needed for the area and customers. As a result of this assessment and consideration, the service competencies for the new welcome center included:

- **Interpersonal Skills** (i.e., training attendants to be flexible, manage stressful situations, and facilitate dialogue);

- **Communication Skills** (i.e., listening, speaking, and writing);

- **Managing the Physical Space** (i.e., assuring that customers and attendants can communicate with limited barriers);

- **Content Knowledge** (training staff to be confident in answering customers' questions);

- **Cross-Cultural** (training staff to understand the value of diversity and recognize any communication barriers that may exist.)

Final Thoughts

Although it takes a great deal of time to identify service competencies, they are not stagnant. For most organizations service competencies are organic and will change over time. For this reason, you must consistently evaluate. For example, you may identify "reliability" as a competency, and even changed your service hours to accommodate customers, but not realize that an academic calendar change opposes your existing hours. For this reason, in order to maintain "reliability" as a service competency, you must modify your practice.

While the hardest part of developing service competencies is the initial creation, ongoing assessment of the relevance of competencies is key. Many service competencies will remain from year to year, but it is likely that some will change on an annual basis. It is crucial that departments evaluate service competencies on an annual basis, or even more. Service competencies should be so broad that the modification of specific application should be fluid and nimble!

SECTION 3: HOW TO SUPPORT FRONTLINE STAFF IN ENHANCING CUSTOMER SERVICE

Lead author for this chapter: Heath Boice-Pardee.

Most offices have a person, or a select few, who consistently offer continuity of service and are often the first people to represent your department and school to internal and external customers. These staff are not usually vice presidents or directors, but staff who work on the frontline of customer interaction. These staff are the faces of your office, the voices over the phone delivering information courteously, and the people answering inquiries efficiently through email. Since frontline staff represent you and your message, as a manager, it is vital that you understand the frontline-specific needs of these vital members of your team.

Likening staff on the "frontline" to military personnel may be considered extreme, yet depending on the day or situation, the daily battle surges in the office environment are real. Constantly barraged with questions, phone calls, and emails that often involve complaints, concerns, and criticisms, frontline staff can experience a variety of skirmishes on a daily basis. For these reasons and many more, providing excellent customer service in higher education settings can be challenging for frontline staff. Understanding the unique circumstances that confront frontline staff each day is key to supporting them and allowing them to excel in providing excellent customer service.

So who do we mean by *frontline staff?* Frontline staff come in a variety of roles from professionals to paraprofessional student employees. Common frontline roles include:

- Staff assistants and office support staff

- Academic advisors

- Residence life staff

- Food service workers

- Custodians

While most college and university personnel work directly with customers in some fashion, the frequency and level of customer interaction for frontline staff is far greater. The increased opportunities for customer interaction come in many forms, which can increase the complexity of providing consistent high-quality service. Additionally, as the first line of customer contact, frontline employees are often at higher risk for managing challenging customers, dealing with conflict, and diffusing situations.

What Support Do Frontline Staff Need?

One of the most challenging aspects of a frontline job, and for some the most rewarding, is managing a wide range of situations and needs. In any given hour on any given day, frontline staff are likely confronted with a variety of needs, wants, and problems from internal and external university customers. A few critical attributes are outlined in this section; however, this is surely not meant to be an exhaustive list.

Triage Frustration and Criticism

As the first point of contact, frontline staff often bear the brunt of customers' frustrations. Since the customer base is diverse in the higher education setting, frontline staff may regularly have contact with students, faculty, staff, parents, community members, alumni, and others. Oftentimes communications from customers, like in many industries, come in the form of complaints. Consider the last time you contacted an organization via telephone, chat, or email to praise them—it wasn't so recently, was it? Most often we reach out to organizations when we have a question, concern, or complaint. In many cases, by the time we actually reach out, we are fueled by frustration and even anger. This is the same at colleges and universities and frontline staff regularly take on the burden of soothing frayed nerves and angry voices. This is an important consideration when determining how to support staff on the front line who triage frustrations and criticisms regularly.

So what is the best way to support frontline staff who triage needs all day long? Here are some simple tips:

- **Back them up.** Since you charge frontline staff with managing sensitive situations, it is important that you support their decisions in front of customers. Even if you need to offer feedback for future ways to tweak a response, it is vital that you show your staff that you support them.

- **Shoulder the burden.** As the manager, you are ultimately responsible for customer satisfaction. When situations get escalated to your level, be sure to take the ball from the frontline staff and take the lead. This will show both your frontline staff and your customer that you are concerned about them.

Being the Face of the Office

Many frontline staff are considered the "face" of an office or department which carries great responsibility. Not only do such staff members need to represent themselves in a positive light, but they must also represent the office, department, division, and even the university to both internal and external customers. While holding this role means that frontline staff have to know institutional priorities, policies, and protocols, it also means that they must put their personal feelings aside and "tow the company line" regardless of their opinion. This can be especially challenging, especially when they have to deliver messages that they don't personally agree with.

Among the many attributes necessary for frontline staff to work productively each day, staying calm in the face of chaos is critical and something that can't easily be taught. This is another attribute that can also be undervalued by managers, but is usually appreciated by customers. In any given hour, frontline staff can be confronted by angry parents, crying students, disillusioned colleagues, malfunctioning equipment, needy bosses, and project deadlines. Remaining calm in the face of pandemonium is critical for providing essential customer service.

The first step in representing an area is for frontline staff to be mindful of tone (e.g., in person, when answering the phone, email, etc.) Tone should always be warm and welcoming, and even cheerful (yes, cheerful). A study at the University of Portsmouth in the United Kingdom revealed that smiles can actually be heard over the phone—meaning, when a person smiles while talking on the phone, their voice and tone changes (Drahota, 2008). Many companies who manage call centers around the world use this tactic to warm-up the tone when greeting frustrated callers.

Here are some tips on how to support frontline staff who are your face and voice each and every day:

- **Share your expectations.** Often staff don't meet our expectations because we don't adequately share them. If there is a specific way that you want your frontline staff to answer the phone, respond to inquiries, or interact with customers, tell them. You may work with them on developing a specific script (see section on Scripting), etc.

- **Give them a break.** Always being "on" can be exhausting, so it's important to provide time away. At the Walt Disney Company, specifically in the theme parks, staff who are working with customers are "on-stage," and those who are not are "off-stage." Be sure that you offer your frontline staff who are "on-stage" regular time "off-stage" so that they can recharge.

Managing Information

Since staff on the frontline are the first points of contact in many departments, they also have access to incredible amounts of information. This means that staff are privy to inside information from many sources about a variety of issues. From which Vice Presidents are good to work for, to the latest health crisis that a director is experiencing, to the student who has to drop out of school for financial reasons, frontline staff are in the know. Managers who develop strong relationships with frontline staff can also benefit from this information by both dispelling rumors and recognizing the importance of campus chatter. Given the abundance of issues that frontline staff face each day, the development of strong university relationships and problem solving skills are vital. Staff must determine the validity of an inquiry or complaint and decide when and to whom to escalate an issue. Staff must also understand a variety of university resources and develop relationships with other office personnel to make appropriate referrals. These skills should be extremely prized and especially regarding relationship building are sometimes under-valued.

Managing large amounts of sensitive information can be a daunting task, managers can support staff by:

- **Maintain open communication.** The more a frontline staffer is connected with information, the more institutional context you gain. Be sure that you maintain an open line of communication with your staff in order to gain insight, and offer institutional context when necessary.

How to Manage the Barriers to Providing Service

Although most frontline staff strive to provide exceptional customer service each day, there are sometimes barriers both in and out of the staff member's control that can inhibit service delivery. This section discusses a few barriers commonly cited by staff and managers alike.

Assess How Physical Space Creates Barriers

While we often focus on people in our quest to provide exceptional customer service, we must not discount the impact of the physical spaces in which we work. The easiest way to assess your physical office environment is to conduct an environmental scan of your area. (For more on this, see Section 6 of this book.)

When you consider the spaces that your students occupy each day, how do they enhance or inhibit interaction with customers?

Having a desk between a frontline staffer and a customer is typical (and in today's sometimes volatile world, sometimes welcomed), but what else gets in the way of interaction? Computer monitors? Counters? Files, folders, or clutter? All of these can inhibit the development of positive customer relations and interactions.

Assess How Policies or Practices Inhibit Service

Are there policies or practices in your office or department that inhibit the delivery of excellent customer service? For example:

- How transparent are your office practices?

- Do students have to make appointments with staff or are there opportunities for walk-ins?

- Are your office hours convenient to your customers? This can be important, especially at lunchtime. Does your office close entirely during lunch, and if so, is this clearly stated to people stopping by?

Surely frontline staff have to abide by and explain policies on a daily basis. Some of the most contentious deal with information that cannot be shared with parents or others, and these often lead to dissatisfaction. However, sharing policies—especially FERPA and other national regulations that prohibit sharing grades or conduct status with parents—can be successfully managed. Through honesty and patience, policies and practices can provide support for how staff respond.

In some cases, policies and practices aren't written anywhere but are part of office history. This leads to how office culture impacts frontline staff providing customer service. Rollins College has instituted a system for identifying unknown obstacles: employees are invited to submit comments on *anything* that slows service. (For more about Rollins College's approach to customer service, see Section 8 of this book.)

How to Manage Office Culture

The culture of a particular office is a significant contributor to the delivery of customer service. Departmental history is often the greatest influencer of culture feeding the "we've always done it that way" mentality. One factor to consider in office culture is *how* frontline staff are empowered to make decisions and what levels of bureaucratic hierarchy have been established. While surely frontline staff aren't hired to make management decisions, having some level of decision making authority can hasten response time and enhance service to customers. An excellent example of this exists within the Walt Disney

Company. At Disney parks, cast members (as employees are called) of every management level have decision-making ability. If a custodian witnesses a child drop an ice cream cone, she/he is empowered to authorize that another cone be scooped free of charge. The same philosophy applies to an office.

What level of decision-making authority have frontline staff been granted? Do they need to obtain management approval for *some* office decisions or *most*? Empowering frontline staff to make decisions will not only improve office morale, but enhance customer service as well.

Survey: Common Concerns for Frontline Staff

One of the best ways to find out how frontline staff are feeling is to ask them, either directly or through the use of an anonymous survey. Some universities have found that a combination of both are most effective in understanding the concerns of frontline staff.

A few years ago I developed an assessment plan at a university to determine how to better support staff on the frontline. The plan incorporated two steps: first an anonymous survey sent to over fifty staff that I reviewed in aggregate, and then, an invitation to groups of frontline staff to discuss the results in person. The following illustrates the questions that were asked, as well as the responses. While we did not conduct a follow-up survey to identify how these specific frontline issues were addressed, subsequent satisfaction increased. Perhaps this was due to simply asking for feedback and conducting personal conversations. Surely based on the responses, some managers made changes.

Consider the following survey and feedback. What changes might *you* make based on the responses?

FRONTLINE STAFF SURVEY

1. What do you perceive to be the greatest challenges of your current position on the frontline? (Check all that apply.)

____ Sufficient training to do my job

____ Physical office environment

____ Dealing with difficult people in person

____ Dealing with difficult people over the phone/ email

____ Dealing with students

____ Micro-managing supervisor

____ Little direction/feedback

____ Managing my own fear/emotions

____ Difficult or uncomfortable office environment

The top responses were:

- Physical office environment

- Micro-managing supervisor

- Little direction/feedback

This illustrates, as previously discussed, how important the physical office environment is to frontline staff. The responses also show that empowerment and supervision are equally important. No one likes to be micromanaged. Establishing a sense of empowerment is crucial to the office environment and to providing good customer service. Additionally, while *micromanagement* isn't preferred, the reverse—inadequate supervision and feedback—is equally problematic.

The second question on the survey helps to identify where to strike the right balance with supervisory support.

FRONTLINE STAFF SURVEY

2. What could your current supervisor do to offer more support? (Check all that apply.)

____ Offer more frequent feedback

____ Offer less feedback

____ Back me up

____ Nothing

The top responses were:

- Offer less feedback

- Nothing

The rationale behind these responses are somewhat perplexing and had to be fleshed-out during the in-person conversations. While surely frontline staff aren't immune to feedback, *too much* can be overpowering. Many frontline staff are truly experts in their field while many managers are not experts on the frontline. According to frontline staff members, being consistently treated as professionals, with regular communication with supervisors is the optimal managerial relationship.

3. In what areas do you feel you need or want additional training? (Check all that apply.)

___ Technology

___ Budgeting

___ Legal issues

___ Student employment issues

___ Time management

___ Mental health issues for students

___ Dealing with difficult students

___ Dealing with difficult faculty/staff

___ Communications skills

___ Calendar/scheduling

___ Ways to support students

___ Writing

___ Managing emotions

The top responses were:

- Legal issues

- Student employment issues

- Time management

- Communications skills

- Calendar/Scheduling

- Managing Emotions

These responses show the breadth and depth of interests and needs of frontline staff. Given the ever-changing legal climate in higher education, staff show concern for university and personal liability when managing issues. As such, frontline staff are eager to stay up to date on legal issues that impact their work, especially regarding Title IX and confidentiality. This can also be associated with student employment issues. Since frontline staff work directly with students, regularly in a supervisory capacity, it is vital that they have accurate employment policy information on a university and even statewide level.

Regarding time management and calendar/scheduling, issues related to these can often be linked with communication skills. Since both of these tasks are primary responsibilities for frontline staff, it is important to communicate with supervisors and customers about specific needs and challenges. Staff who are responsible for managing meetings that involve high-level managers, faculty, or issues can find these meetings challenging to coordinate. Communicating this difficulty shouldn't be a reflection on skill, but an office reality that needs to be managed. In conversations, many frontline staff noted that they often get blamed for logistical challenges outside of their control. The best solution for this is support and understanding.

Communication skills can also be related to managing emotions. Given the high-level administrative responsibilities that many frontline staff have, the consistent and sometimes challenging interactions with customers, and competing priorities, emotional impact can be great.

Having the understanding and support of managers can ease some of the pressure felt on the frontline and one of the best ways to achieve this is through direct honest communication.

FRONTLINE STAFF SURVEY

4. What is the part of your job that you enjoy most? (Check all that apply.)

____ Working/dealing with students

____ Problem solving

____ Scheduling appointments

____ Hours/schedule

____ Interaction with other departments

____ Type of work

____ Lunch

The top responses were:

- Problem solving

- Scheduling appointments

- Hours/schedule

- Lunch

According to my conversations with frontline staff, many enjoy the challenges of solving the myriad of problems that arise minute-to-minute and scheduling appointments to help achieve departmental goals. These factors point back to the strong abilities many frontline staff possess and their pride in helping achieve goals.

As for hours/schedule, many frontline staff work a traditional 9:00 a.m. to 5:00 p.m. (or 8:30 a.m. to 4:30 p.m.) schedule without evening or weekend hours, which is appealing. Additionally, some staff note that they have flexibility in their schedules in order to attend to family commitments, personal appointments, etc., which makes managing their time a bit easier. As for lunch being an enjoyable part of the day, this shouldn't be surprising. This response does not mean that frontline staff can't wait to stop working, but they surely do need a break in the day. In my conversations, frontline staff enjoy the opportunity during their lunch time to run errands, take a walk, catch-up with friends, and, well, eat lunch.

Finally, I asked frontline staff the following open-ended question:

FRONTLINE STAFF SURVEY

5. What is one aspect of your current job description that you feel is incorrect or does not fit your position?

The top responses were:

- "I'm not allowed to problem-solve."

- "Multi-tasking is an understatement."

- "Micro-management!"

All of these items have been addressed in previous sections of this chapter. Frontline staff are professionals who enjoy utilizing their leadership skills and talents to juggle situations. As such, staff enjoy the freedom to make decisions and exercise their skills in an effort to provide excellent service to both internal and external customers.

How Managers Can Support Frontline Staff

Given the multitude of frontline staff responsibilities, it is vital that managers create support systems that promote self-care. It is important for frontline staff to feel supported and empowered to take care of themselves. For some who feel that their primary responsibility is providing care and service to others every day, self-care can be difficult to fit into a busy schedule. This is why it is important for supervisors of frontline staff to actively be aware of the levels of activity and stress in the office and encourage staff to ease tension.

Following or Creating Policies/Office Procedures

For frontline staff who are hourly, many colleges and universities follow state policies regarding mandatory breaks and lunchtimes. These should be strictly followed. Some schools even develop office policies not allowing staff to eat lunch at their desks, which can be met with discontent by those on the frontline. While some frontline staff find such policies restrictive, the rationale encourages staff to take a true break. In my own experience as a manager, I am not good at making lunchtime sacred. Even if I see frontline staffers sitting at their desk eating lunch, it's not out of the realm of possibility for me to follow-up on a question, hand-off a project, or discuss an ongoing issue. If the staff are not at their desks, managers like me will have to wait to get a response, or find the answers ourselves, and that is perfectly acceptable!

Even if frontline staff do not want to leave their desk for lunch, they should surely be encouraged to leave their desk. Managers should encourage frontline staff to take a walk, grab coffee with a colleague, or even go to the fitness center or library. The important part is that frontline staff have the opportunity to disengage or vent for 30-60 minutes. This will allow a bit of time to recharge before diving back in to deal with office stress.

Providing Professional Development

When many of us think of providing professional development opportunities for staff, we often think of national conferences such as NASPA, NACADA, or others for new, mid-level, or seasoned administrators. We sometimes forget about finding opportunities that will engage frontline staff. Depending on the role of the frontline staff, professional development opportunities may vary. As a manager, it is important to consider the needs of frontline staff as you would any other professional. Professional development opportunities could consist of on-campus trainings, regional day programs, or national conferences. You might also consider signing up for a membership at a regional, statewide, or national organization that usually offers regular training opportunities.

If there isn't something that fits your budget or schedule, there are numerous webinars offered that can be viewed individually or projected to a large group across campus. This way, campus departments can share the cost and the opportunity for frontline staff to discuss interdepart-mentally. Topics of interest might include:

- Project management,

- Dealing with difficult customers,

- Proactive problem solving, and more.

If budgets are simply too tight, managers may encourage frontline staff to identify a self-help or professional development book that meets their needs and interests. This is likely something that most departments can fund and staff may feel encouraged that managers are considering their needs.

Develop a "Shadow Team"

Consider This...

Managers may consider creating a frontline shadow team that consists of frontline staffers from a variety of departments. Empower the team to schedule observations for each of the departments represented to gain insight on:

- Customer traffic flow

- Physical space

- Routine office practices

When the visits are finished, teams can meet to discuss the observations, identify what went well, and gather ideas for improvement. Empowering "shadow teams" costs little—but provides priceless opportunities for empowering your staff to improve service!

An idea that some campuses have employed, which typically doesn't cost a dime, is interdepartmental shadowing on the frontline. In a shadowing program, frontline staff from a variety of departments spend some time in a different area for a few hours, a morning, or a day. These opportunities allow staff to see what others experience, and give frontline staff a chance to discuss and share strategies and expertise with each other.

Shadowing opportunities not only offer prospects for idea-sharing, but showcase and acknowledge staffers' expertise with each other and enhance relationships around campus. All of these benefits will enhance morale and service to customers!

A quick step you can take—even without a "shadow team" in place—is to invite a colleague from another office to visit yours.

We go to our office every day and often become oblivious to how our office spaces, especially our reception areas, *look* and *feel* to customers.

Invite your colleague—who doesn't work in your office area everyday—to visit as though it's the first time. They should experience your space, services, etc. as a customer. Hand them the worksheet on the next page or ask them for feedback on similar questions.

OBSERVATION VISIT

Upon entering the office, the first thing I noticed was:

_____

_____

_____

One aspect of the office that *facilitates* service is:

_____

_____

_____

One aspect of the office that is a *barrier* to service is (e.g., consider placement of computer screen, desk placement, wall units, etc.)

_____

_____

_____

_____

This office makes me feel:

_____

_____

_____

_____

Consider This...

Ask without Intruding

It's never wrong to ask how someone is doing. While some managers are hesitant to comingle work and personal life, sometimes it is essential to do just that. If a staff member suddenly acts differently (e.g., quiet, withdrawn, impatient), you may consider asking one of these questions:

"Tom, I've noticed you've been quiet lately. Is everything all right?"

"Mary, it seems as though something is bothering you. Is there anything I can do to support you?"

While these questions might elicit a variety of responses, at least the staff member will know that you are concerned and willing to offer support.

Advocating Self-Care

In addition to encouraging and supporting opportunities for professional development for frontline staff, self-care is something else that should be considered. Like all of us, frontline staff must juggle professional and personal needs simultaneously but the daily stress of persistent customer interaction can be taxing.

Sometimes what a frontline staff member needs in order to maintain a high level of customer service are identifying ways to "escape" from the daily workflow. This means that stepping away from the office and providing opportunities to "forget" about the work is important. Is there a yoga class that a frontline staffer has always wanted to attend, but just needs an opportunity or encouragement to do so? Managers should ask and identify ways to make such opportunities accessible during the workday.

Additionally, it is important to consider that sometimes frontline staff members are managing personal issues that have nothing to do with work. These challenges can vary from personal health management to dealing with a family member or not having adequate childcare. Has a staff member shared a personal struggle at home? As a manager, have you asked if there is something that you can do to support your frontline staff? Most colleges and universities have resources available for employees struggling with personal issues, and it is essential for managers to emphasize resources.

Holding Up the Mirror

One key to providing thoughtful customer service is being transparent. In order to facilitate transparency, it is important that we know ourselves. Knowing my strengths, weaknesses, hot-buttons, soft spots, and more will allow me to understand how I can best deliver information and messages to customers. To advance this exercise, it is also helpful for you to compare your personal notes with others around you (e.g., co-workers, supervisors, etc.) to see if your view of yourself matches the impressions you leave with people.

Surely this sounds intimidating, and holding up a mirror to our behaviors can be scary, but the benefits will likely provide new insight into your skills and how you can enhance your image with customers of all sorts, including co-workers.

SELF-AUDITING YOUR OWN CUSTOMER SERVICE

DIRECTIONS

On the left of each item, rank yourself:

1 means "needs improvement."
3 means "most of the time/usually."
5 means "always/consistently."

Then, have a supervisor or coworker rank you on each item. Copy their answers to the right. Then review and compare—and most importantly, discuss the results.

Self-Score (1-5)	Item	Colleague-Assigned Score (1-5)
_____	Always polite with customers in person/on the phone/email	_____
_____	Accepts feedback about dept. processes/policies well	_____
_____	Works to exceed customer expectations	_____
_____	Tries not to shuffle customers from place to place	_____

SELF-AUDITING YOUR OWN CUSTOMER SERVICE

1 means "needs improvement."
3 means "most of the time/usually."
5 means "always/consistently."

Self-Score (1-5)	Item	Colleague-Assigned Score (1-5)
_____	Provides accurate information to customers	_____
_____	Makes customers feel welcome	_____
_____	Makes customers feel special	_____
_____	Follows-up with customers as promised	_____
_____	Provides "service with a smile," while managing personal challenges	_____
_____	Does not let personal issues impact service excellence	_____
_____	Is knowledgeable about departmental policies	_____
_____	Is knowledgeable about our larger organization	_____
_____	Responds to customer inquiries in a timely manner	_____
_____	Appropriately hands off customer concerns to manager	_____
_____	Prioritizes customers' needs	_____
_____	Takes a break as appropriate when frazzled	_____

1 means "needs improvement."
3 means "most of the time/usually."
5 means "always/consistently."

	Doesn't "gossip" about customers freely	
_____		_____
_____	_____ (Add your own!) _____	_____
_____	_____	_____
_____	_____	_____
_____	_____	_____
_____	_____	_____

Final Thoughts

Frontline staff have a variety of needs in order to maintain high levels of service quality. From dealing with difficult callers, upset parents, or keeping up with email and scheduling, staff on the frontline are hammered throughout each day with a wide array of situations. As managers, it is important to maintain high-levels of communication with frontline staff in order to better understand the complexities and challenges of each workday. Increased communication will likely result in deeper dialogue on what challenges the office is facing and what is needed to support those on the frontline to meet, and exceed, expectations for customer service.

SECTION 4: SCRIPTING AND SERVICE EXCELLENCE

Lead author for this chapter: Eileen Soisson.

Scripting can help you in customer service operations to ensure consistency of service delivery, and best practices can immediately be seen within the airline and hospitality industries. Airlines use this to provide safety instructions at the beginning of a flight or a farewell message to their customers. Resorts and theme parks use scripting to answer questions that potential and incoming guests commonly ask about the resort, park, or choice destination.

Scripting is now also more common within areas of higher education that provide frontline service. The Office of Student Accounts may use a script when a service representative answers the phone; the Office of Admissions may use a script to answer questions regarding residency laws; the Registrar's Office may use it to cover necessary items with in-person interactions. Scripting helps design and manage the service interaction between the university representative and its customer. Universities are starting to recognize the benefits of using a practice from other service-oriented universities within operations, and we anticipate seeing more of this as service programs become more prevalent in higher education.

What is Scripting?

"Thank you for calling Coastal Carolina University, this is Eileen. How may I help you today?"

We have all heard some form of this greeting when calling somewhere, and while this may sound like just another way to answer the phone, there has been some scripting involved with this greeting. The person answering the phone was most likely trained on a proper way to answer the phone and the words to say upon answering calls.

Scripting offers an employee a time-saving guide to follow when interacting with customers, whether that be over the telephone, email, or in person. A script for a simple type of service activity like answering the phone may provide a variety of acceptable and appropriate things to say when answering the phone. A script can also be more detailed in order to answer a particular question or address a specific customer concern. This type of script would include step-by-step directives about how to address each part of the service interaction and its necessary actions.

The use of service scripts provides an assurance of a particular service quality level by employees (Leidner 1993, Stewart 2003). If a script is designed and used effectively, this service tool helps treat customers in a way that best represents the mission and purpose of your office/department/university. A script can harm the service process and produce a negative response from the customer if it is written in such a way that sounds robotic or isn't flexible enough to be helpful.

Why We Use Scripting

Effective scripting:

- Provides quality and consistent service levels for customers

- Provides confidence and comfort level for employees

- Creates a more branded image for the university

- Reinforces the service culture

The pre-written conversation provides everyone with the same tool and standard to use when answering the phone, responding to an email, and/or engaging in one-on-one interactions in certain situations. A script ensures that all employees will address a situation with the same information, allowing for a more consistent service level for all customers. In certain areas – such as legality, compliance, policy, and procedures – a script is an ideal service tool to use for compliance and consistency.

Providing a script can also help employees feel more confident and comfortable during an interaction since the proper way to handle the situation has already been provided. The early preparation allows the employee to focus on the customer and his or her issue rather than worrying about the "right thing" to say. The script helps the employee know how to guide the conversation and respond appropriately throughout, taking away some of the fear of the unknown. As an example, think of a new employee who is learning all there is to learn within his or her area; one day, he/she gets asked about FERPA and is not sure of the exact way to explain the federal law and the institution's policy. The script will allow him or her to provide a clear answer and set up a better service interaction.

Scripting reinforces that service-oriented brand image for customers calling the university. Scripts help set the tone for your institution. When that college representative follows the script and uses the university name every time he or she answers the phone, there is a reinforcement of the university's branding through pleasant and professional service. In order for the institution to make a positive and memorable moment of truth, that phone call must be answered in a way that represents the service strategy of the institution and provides an indication of how service will be delivered in future interactions.

Can Customers Tell When You Are Using a Script?

Three studies will help us explore the customer's perspective with regard to the use of a script in service interactions. We will share two studies from the University of Utah's David Eccles School of Business (DESB) in 2012, as well as a survey done by Hello Operator, to see if customers can really tell when you are using a script and how that makes them feel (Borowski, 2014).

A team including Don Wardell (professor and chair of the David Eccles School of Business' Department of Operations and Information Systems), Bryan Bonner (DESB management professor), Rohit Verma (former University of Utah professor, currently of Cornell University); and Liana Victorino (former Utah Ph.D. student, currently at the University of Victoria) have had their studies published: "Can Customers Detect Script Usage in the Service Encounter?" (*Journal of Service Research*) and "Scripting the Service Encounter: A Customer's Perspective of Quality," a study done by Wardell, Verma, and Victorino (*Production and Operations Management*). The studies were conducted by having people watch a video of a realistic customer encounter in a real hotel. This approach added an authenticity to the experiment and provided respondents with a real-world experience that they could genuinely respond to rather than answering questions to a written case study.

The studies revealed that customers are extremely savvy in recognizing when they are being delivered a script in a service encounter, and that they don't mind as long as the encounter involves a relatively standardized interaction, like checking into a hotel. However, the studies also indicated that if organizations heavily script an encounter in which the customer is looking for specific, customized information—say, a restaurant recommendation from a hotel concierge—they risk making customers feel like they're getting diminished service quality.

"They want the interaction to feel sincere and natural, and not feel robotic," Wardell shared. "They want to feel like the person cares about their request and that they're being treated as individuals, not some mass-produced commodity." This study also found that the skill of improvisation during the call, while staying true to the message and mission, was important in a positive image of the call and results.

Hello Operator surveyed a random sample of 500 U.S. adults in 2015 to learn more about the perceptions of call centers and the impact of the use of scripts during interactions. More than two-thirds of the respondents said their perception of the customer service delivery improves when the agent doesn't sound like they are reading from a script. According to the survey, customers expect there to be a level of care that comes through the phone or any interaction, and often scripts are written to include lines of understanding. We can use such lines as "I understand this can be a very frustrating time of the semester," and "This recent change in the residency law can be very overwhelming and difficult to understand..."

We want to use the script as a tool to enhance the experience, not one that focuses too heavily on what the service representative should be saying. If we can help a customer along the way from a place of understanding, the scripting and phrasing will likely progress more organically.

Consider This...

Manners

The importance of using manners is shown in the survey question responses below from Hello Operator:

Which of the following makes you feel like a customer service agent really cares about your call?

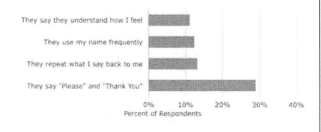

Lessons learned:

- Yes, customers can detect subtleties in scripting approaches in different service situations.

- Customers want to feel like the person cares about their request and that they're being treated and listened to as individuals.

- Scripts are a great guide. The most effective scripts allow for improvisation and are designed to match the type of service encounter.

A Script That Provides Service Excellence

The broad goal of any service program within a university—to improve customer interactions that support student success and the institutional mission—requires compromise. That compromise comes in the form of creating scripts and scripting strategies that strive to standardize customer service within the university's guidelines and policies, while at the same time allowing for individual care and personal service.

Knowing that customers do not mind the use of scripting, but that they *do* mind the lack of human experience and ability to go off-script, we can see where compromise is needed. Service representatives or agents obviously can't be given free rein to handle students, parents, alumni, etc., however they please, but it should be recognized that scripts leaving no room for improvisation can lead to failure in customer service. Take the time to identify areas of the script where an ad lib or personal interjection are completely acceptable and encouraged.

Scripting must be intentional and must take into account the time needed to allow customers to speak and respond appropriately. The script level must match the level of the service encounter and provide appropriate levels of empowerment and/or responsibility with the options. For example, if the script is designed to assist with answering the phone, the level is rather elementary and the script might include four options of how to answer the phone. However, if the service encounter was more advanced, then the steps would need to be more detailed in order to effectively respond to the question/situation.

Scripts that provide service excellence:

> …are taught in training.

> …have an open and a close.

> …address a typical service concern or procedure with appropriate verbiage to follow.

> … are solution-based and include options.

> … are designed with the customer response in mind.

Scripts that do not provide service excellence:

> …are used as the only way to communicate with the customer.

> …are an ongoing monologue and not spoken aloud/tested to be conversational.

> …prompt employees to simply read words off a

screen or paper/manual and not include any interaction.

…make customers feel more like a number than an actual human being.

Consider This...

A Guideline

When the benefit of a scripted line is minimal, or when it does not outweight the displeasure customers feel when speaking with staff who are obviously following a script to the letter, that line should not be included in a script.

Telephone Service Scripts

Telephone scripts provide the appropriate standard, verbiage, and flow of a telephone conversation. They can be typed out or they can include bullet points that allow the service representative the opportunity to cover the necessary service steps while still letting their own personality come through. In order for a service script to be effective over the telephone, there needs to be a welcoming greeting and gracious closing, response to appropriate questions, and a sincere apology if necessary. The script must also be tested to be customer-friendly.

Telephone Greetings

When answering the telephone, it is important to use an upbeat opening and a smile to set a positive tone and represent the department well. The person on the other end of the line represents a service opportunity, so be sure the tone of the greeting conveys a readiness to assist, rather than conveying that the call is an interruption. As simple as it sounds, add "smile" as the first step in the script.

The telephone greeting should not be extremely long, so use good judgement with how much sounds like too much. The opening script should quickly establish the name of the institution, department name, the name of the live representative, and an offer of assistance. It should be concise, direct, polite, and should easily lead into the customer concern or need. If the telephone greeting requires a breath in between, it is too long.

1. **Acknowledge value:** Thank the customer for calling; communicate an appreciation for them calling YOU and offer to assist them right then and there.

2. **University and employee identification:** Stating the university's name in the introduction assures the person they have called the right place and also promotes the brand of the university. Personalize the conversation and create accountability by identifying who you are. Be sure to mention the name of your department so the caller knows which department they have reached.

3. **Offer assistance:** Ask the customer how they can be helped and do so in genuine tone and delivery. Please note there is a difference between "How may I help you?" and "Can I help you?" The former indicates that you are there to help, but just need the specifics of how to do that. The latter is asking if you have the capacity or ability to help the customer, and for that, you may get the sassy response of, "I don't know, can you?" In order to provide the best opening possible, ask the

caller directly **how** you may help them to establish that is your No. 1 priority during the phone call. Here are some examples to consider:

Telephone Service Excellence Examples

- "Hello, and thank you for calling (name of college). My name is (name of representative) with (Career Services). How may I help you today?"

- "Thank you for calling (XYZ College), this is (Eileen) with (Career Services). How may I help you today?"

- "Good (morning/afternoon/evening), this is Cara with PSU's Alumni Chapter in (Raleigh); how may I help you today?

What is NOT Service Excellence?

- "This is Taylor." (Unless this is an internal call and Taylor recognizes the caller.)

- "ABC UNIVERSITY!!!!!!!!!" (No one likes to be shouted at.)

- "Admissions Office."

- Any of the above with gum or figurative marbles in the mouth.

Consider This...

Holiday/Seasonal Greetings

Greetings can be made more personal during the seasons to reflect the time of year:

"Happy Holidays from ABC University Housing. This is Steve. How may I help you?"

Or, at Coastal Carolina University on any Tuesday:

"Happy Teal Tuesday from CCU. This is Nick. How may I help you?"

Exercise!

Sample Telephone Script

Fill in the telephone script below for your institution:

"Hello, and thank you for calling
_____. My name is
_____ with _____.
How may I help you today?"

Service Suggestion: Write your personal greeting on a notecard or post-it note and keep it right next to your phone until you get accustomed to saying it every time you answer a call.

Transfer the Call

There will be times when a caller must be transferred to another person or department better able to address his/her question or concern. Higher education institutions of all sizes face the service issue of the caller being sent around to several departments before getting to the one they need. For example, the caller needs to talk to someone in the Admissions Office, but instead they are routed to Financial Aid, Financial Services, and Student Health Services due to a misunderstanding of the caller's issue by each of the agents taking the call. This can become known as the "ABC College Shuffle" – whether that is on the telephone or in-person service. The shuffle commonly happens when employees are not sure where to send someone, so they pick a location that sounds like they may have something to do with that academic situation, call there, and pass the customer along the way until they are shuffled to their final destination on campus.

In order to lessen the number of touchpoints a customer has and to avoid this "shuffle," take this service opportunity to use a "warm transfer." In a warm transfer, you provide the other representative you are transferring the customer to with the pertinent information and appropriate emotion before the handoff takes place. Offer assurance to the caller as you share who it is the caller is being sent to and why. Explain the credentials of the department or person so the caller understands the purpose behind the transfer (especially if they have already been transferred multiple times), and that you are transferring the caller to a subject matter expert in the area they have a question/ concern/problem about.

1. **Explain the why** – Politely explain the reason why you need to transfer to someone else (i.e., wrong number, wrong department,

another area would be more informed to answer the call, etc.) and reinforce that you are not simply passing the caller off to someone else.

2. **Provide contact information** – Provide your name and extension in case there is a disconnection or in case the caller needs to get back in touch later, as well as the person/department name you are connecting the caller to and his/her extension number for the same reasons.

3. **Ask permission** – Ask for permission to make the transfer and allow the caller a chance to ask any last questions before the transfer is initiated. Once they have granted permission to be transferred, politely ask for permission place them on hold while you make the transfer.

4. **Provide information** – Share the information and details gathered thus far with the employee accepting the transferred call so that he/she is up to speed with the situation.

5. **Make introduction** – Return to the caller and introduce the name and/or department of the person to whom you will be transferring the call. Provide assurance that the caller will be taken care of from here on out and ask if there is anything still needed.

6. **Complete the transfer** – Connect callers and be sure to hang up on your end.

Service Excellence Example:

"I would be happy to transfer you to (Sally) in (Career Services); the reason I am sending you specifically to (Sally) is because (she oversees all the internships and would know exactly what employer paperwork you would need to complete to post an open management position with your business). (Sally's) extension is (2686) should we get disconnected or should you need to call her back in the near future."

What is NOT Service Excellence?

- "Hold please." (Transfer call)

- "I'm not paid enough to transfer calls."

- "Sure." (Transfer)

Consider This...

Hold Music

A university that takes advantage of each opportunity also evaluates and is intentional about its hold music. Does the university hold music capture the brand? Promote upcoming events? (Note: The alma mater is a better choice for hold music than outdated or potentially offensive music.)

Exercise!

Sample Telephone Script

Fill in the telephone script below for your institution:

"I would be happy to transfer you to _____ (person) in _____ (department). The reason I am going to transfer you to _____ (person) is because _____ (subject matter expert justification).

"Does that help? (Allow time for confirmation or denial, and provide the appropriate response.) Their number is _____ (#) should they not be in or if you want to follow up in the future; and should you and I get disconnected and there is need to speak again, my number is _____ (#). Before I transfer you to _____ (person/department), is there anything else I can assist you with? (Leave appropriate time for them to really think and respond. If *yes*, assist them with their question or concern. If *no*, proceed to transfer.)

"At this time I am going to transfer you. Have a great day!"

Telephone Apology

A sincere apology goes a long way in any service interaction, whether in higher education or any other field. In higher education, there is such a high ticket price on the cost of education that itis vital we pay attention to how we apologize. Here are a few best practices to get started:

1. Be sincere in the apology.

2. Explain what happened and *why*.

3. Acknowledge the customer's pain or inconvenience; use empathy statements.

4. Explain the future steps and use the pronoun "we" to show there is a togetherness in how we are going to move forward. This is especially important if this is a situation between a student and a staff/faculty member so that there is a level of trust established.

5. Provide legitimate and sincere assurance.

To unhappy customers who are looking for solutions, an apology—although appreciated—is usually not enough. Instead, include in your script the phrase "I can take care of that for you," and then empower your service agents to actually resolve issues. Customers who contact call centers expect more than just someone to take the blame; they expect that their problems will be solved—and quickly. By designing a script that makes it clear that the live representatives are capable of resolving problems directly, you diffuse a number of problematic situations before they start and help to turn potentially negative experiences into positive ones.

Service Excellence Examples:

- "I can't explain it, but I can apologize for it."

- "I apologize for the delay in response but I have the information you requested now and am happy to discuss and answer any questions."

- "I apologize for the hold; I was speaking with my supervisor to be sure I had the correct information for your unique situation."

What is NOT Service Excellence?

- "I'm sorry you feel that way."

- "Too bad, so sad."

- "That's our policy."

Telephone Closing

- Recap what was accomplished.

- Explain what happens next and any action steps required by either person on the phone.

- Ask if anything is still needed before ending the call (be intentional).

- Extend a personal thank you using the caller's name.

- Invite the caller to get in touch with future needs.

- End with a courteous phrase.

Once the problem has been effectively resolved, the agent should ask if there is anything else that the customer would like addressed, thank them for taking the time to call, restate the institution's name, and then politely sign off. Much like the opening script, this should be done in a concise way—the customer, at this point, is hopefully satisfied and will probably be eager to bring the call to a close.

Service Excellence Example:

"Is there anything else that I can help you with today? (Wait for response; address any additional concerns.) In that case, thank you for calling (name of college/ department). We hope that you got the answers/direction you needed, and we look forward to working with you/seeing you on campus/having your family here/etc. in the future. Have a great day!"

What is NOT Service Excellence?

- "Bye." (Click of the telephone)

- "Un-huh, have a good day."

- "See ya."

Voicemail Greeting

If a caller ends up in an employee's voice mailbox, the outgoing message should be professional and easy to understand. It should consist of the following components:

1. Initial greeting.

2. Statement that explains why you're unable to take the call.

3. Invitation to leave a message.

4. Response time for you to get back to the caller.

5. Provide an alternative means to get hold of you, or provide another person the caller can get hold of in your absence (if applicable).

Service Suggestion: At the end of the voicemail message, add a "Go Chants!" or "We Are...Penn State" or whatever is the school spirit slogan to support the school and community!

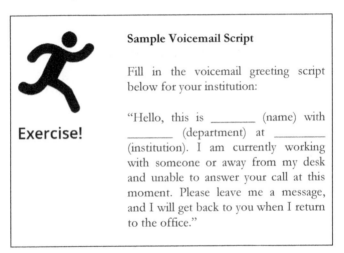

Exercise!

Sample Voicemail Script

Fill in the voicemail greeting script below for your institution:

"Hello, this is _____ (name) with _____ (department) at _____ (institution). I am currently working with someone or away from my desk and unable to answer your call at this moment. Please leave me a message, and I will get back to you when I return to the office."

Email Service Scripts

Scripts can be used within the written version of communication and provide text for the employee. In departments and colleges, there are several questions that are asked constantly and consistently throughout the day, and it is important that the answer be provided in a way that can later referenced and must be correct.

Are scripts really used within higher education? The Dean of Students Office at Coastal Carolina University has developed more than 100 letter templates used as scripts utilizing a case management software to document incidents and information regarding student conduct, behavior, advocacy, and intervention. The office created scripts regarding regular processes and concerns in order to have consistent and efficient communication with students. These templates require little to no editing by the sender and assist with service efficiency.

Steps to remember when using a script with emails:

1. Greet the customer.

2. Thank them for reaching out.

3. Summarize the situation.

4. Answer the question/concern.

5. Use tools to help explain and support—such as screenshots, step-by-step lists, links, etc.

6. Close with style and professionalism (double check your work).

7. Be sure to use a professional signature file that includes your name, title, department, and updated contact information (include physical location).

Email Script Examples:

The following are three examples of email scripts and templates used with the Office of Admissions and Merit Awards.

EMAIL SCRIPT 1

(Insert name)

I am delighted to hear of your interest in Coastal Carolina University! CCU offers a number of exciting academic programs combined with a variety of student organizations and activities providing students with an experience that proves to be both academically stimulating and socially engaging.

We will open our application for the fall of 2018 this September. In the meantime, I would encourage you to schedule your visit to CCU's campus. We offer tours Monday through Friday at 9:30 a.m. This September, we will also offer tours at 2 p.m. You can register at:

http://www.coastal.edu/admissions/visits.html.

Please let me know if you have any additional questions.

(Your name)

EMAIL SCRIPT 2

Subject: Response Required by July 7

Deploy to 17/FA AC FF with no OR

From: (insert name)

Important Notice

Welcome to Coastal Carolina University! I am writing because you have not completed your enrollment process, and it is important that you complete this process to officially become a Chanticleer.

Orientation begins one week from today. All new students are required to attend an Orientation session, and our records indicate you have not registered for a session yet.

All sessions are still open. Make sure you register today. You can register online at: www.coastal.edu/nsfp/orientation/nso/ or you can call _____ (#) to register over the phone. You will need your WebAdvisor username and password to register online. If you need help logging into WebAdvisor, please contact the Office of Admissions and Merit Awards at admissions2@coastal.edu or call _____. (#)

Please contact me if you have questions or concerns. You can reach me by email at (email address) or call (phone number).

If you have recently registered for Orientation, please disregard this notice.

If your plans have changed and you no longer plan to attend Coastal Carolina University this fall, please email admissions2@coastal.edu with your request to withdraw your application.

I look forward to welcoming you and your family to CCU this summer.

Best wishes,

(Name)

P.S. Don't miss your chance to join #TEALnation. Register for Orientation today!

EMAIL SCRIPT 3

Subject: Beat the Dec. 1 Priority Deadline

Deploy 11/30/16 to 17/FA FF prospects

Remember, our Priority Application Deadline is December 1. If we receive your online application, your high school transcript, and your ACT or SAT test scores by this deadline, you could have your admissions decision before the end of the year. You'll still have until May 1 to make your decision to attend Coastal Carolina University. So apply to CCU today!

Are you taking the SAT or ACT in December? You can still apply before December 1. Just include your scheduled test dates on your application and list Coastal Carolina University as one of the test score recipients. We'll use the scores to evaluate your application as soon as we receive them.

We encourage you to visit our campus if you haven't already. To schedule your campus tour, please go to www.coastal.edu/visit or call 800.277.7000.

EMAIL SCRIPT 3, CONTINUED

We look forward to working with you. Please call us at 800.277.7000 if you have any questions about the application or the application process.

Don't miss the December 1 priority deadline. Apply online today!

Best wishes!

(Name)

P.S. If you've recently applied, don't worry, we've got your application. Just email admissions@coastal.edu and we'll update our files.

How Would You Rate Your Email Communication?

On a scale of 1-10, 10 being the best, how would you rate your service provided through email communication? How would your colleagues rate it? Creating a script for emails can be useful tool for *both* internal and external communication.

Consider This...

In-Person Service Moments

There is nothing better than a campus face-to-face service interaction that "wins the day!" Coastal Carolina University's University Recreation department created a mantra to live by and serve others with in the spring of 2013: #WinTheDay! This is used with student workers to provide motivation and build winning attitudes, an experience that will ultimately be felt by anyone they come in contact with during their work shifts and beyond.

To better illustrate this concept, Jody Davis, director of University Recreation at CCU shared these comments:

"We try and hashtag all of our boards with the #WinTheDay! saying, and any motivational quotes we use end with the hashtag #WinTheDay! We periodically hand out stickers that say #WinTheDay! We want our employees to have a winning attitude; we discuss this at length in our Feel the Teal interviews. We want all of our patrons to feel like winners when they arrive and when they exit the facility. We can only accomplish this by setting up a culture of winning. (The winning is not targeted to compete with others, but winning the day for ourselves, so we can be a better version of ourselves.) Our student employees are trained on the small things such as speaking, making eye contact, smiling, and going the extra mile. College-aged students love enthusiasm, and the fist-pumping #WinTheDay mantra fulfills that part of the culture. #WinTheDay helps us in executing our mission, which, in a condensed version, is student success."

This university department has created a culture where in-person moments are guided by a mantra or a theme. Perhaps your institution is not there yet and needs a start. Begin by creating a list of multiple acceptable greetings and approaches to assisting with difficult in-person situations so that employees feel comfortable and can select an option that best matches their personality and style.

In-Person Greetings

If you are the first one to greet someone entering your department or office area, be proactive so the customer does not feel as if they are interrupting someone when asking for help or assistance. Remember, as a frontline person, you represent not only the department but the entire institution.

1. Provide a warm welcome with open body language.

2. Introduce yourself and area of the college you represent.

3. Offer any assistance and ask probing questions to clarify need.

4. Use phrases that support the goal of making everyone feel welcome and included in your area of service.

5. Establish a rapport to personalize the greeting.

6. Remind them of your name and area in case they should need service again. (Provide a business card, if applicable.)

In-Person Greeting Service Excellence Examples:

* "Hello!/Hi!"

* "Good morning/afternoon/evening!"

- "Welcome to _____!"

- "Hi, Mr./Mrs. _____. It's great to see you again."

- "I'm pleased to meet you." (When introduced to a customer.)

- "What can I help you with today?"

- "Can I help you find something/someone in our office?"

- "Hello, my name is _____. May I ask your name?"

- "How may I help you today?"

What is NOT Service Excellence?

- "What do you need?" (Followed by a long and agonizing sigh.)

- "??????" (Picture a perplexed or confused look here.)

- "It's my first day, so I hope you don't need anything special."

- "Yes?" (While eating at the desk.)

- Prolonged silence while continuing to type.

Taking the HEAT

For any employee working in higher education, there will be a time that you are going to have to respond and assist with a difficult situation. That situation may involve a student, parent, alumni, or fellow employee at the university and each situation is unique because of the individuality of the person bringing you the situation. How we approach any difficult situation is important and that includes the attitude we bring to the situation. A difficult situation is an opportunity to make something right and needs to be approached as a chance to assist, rather than as something to "deal with." Think about it: When we say, "I had to deal with this customer today..." or "*you* go deal with her," there is a negative connotation. Let's try to avoid thinking, and then saying, the customer is something to "deal with," and instead see those difficult situations as opportunities. The more experience you gain with difficult situations, the more prepared you are to handle and assist with the next one. And there **will** be a next one.

During a customer interaction, there may the possibility that the person feels unsatisfied or unhappy with how things have been handled thus far, and you will be the lucky person who gets to assist and try to make the situation right. This four-step method will help prepare someone to assist with a difficult situation or person. Although this is not considered a script per se, this is a great guiding tool when having to focus on results while emotions present an obstacle to thinking clearly.

This four step model known as "Taking the HEAT" will help you during a difficult situation:

H – Hear the customer out. Take the time to listen to what the person is saying. Try to resist interrupting the person, no matter how much you know the answer or want them to stop talking. Dale Carnegie tells us in *How to Win Friends and Influence People* that when you interrupt someone, it adds three more minutes on to their rant. Also think about it—if you interrupt someone three times, that is nine minutes that could have been spent working on results.

E – Empathize. The best way to show empathy in customer service is to repeat back to the customer what you hear and add some care and compassion. Make sure that you get the customer to confirm or deny that is indeed the problem that needs to be solved. For example – "What I am hearing is that you are upset because all of your classes got dropped. Is that right?"

A – Apologize if needed, and include "the ask." Studies show that when you ask the consumer how to make a situation right, they are more likely to provide a solution that costs less money and takes less time.

Note: We don't apologize for a policy because that is non-negotiable and something that can't be changed.

T – Take action. Make sure that someone does something. This step must take the most amount of time. Assure the customer that you indeed are equipped to assist with this situation. Provide information as to what is going to happen, by whom, by when, any necessary follow up, etc.

Keep HEAT close to the phone, or wherever you may confront a difficult situation, and use it to walk through your responses until it becomes natural and part of the institution's culture.

Play Out the Service Interaction

In his book *9 Things You Simply Must Do*, Dr. Henry Cloud encourages people to play out the movie of their lives. This applies to a service interaction taking place face to face. Play out the entire service interaction and ask yourself how you want this to end. If this were in a movie, would people be happy with the ending? What would the music sound like after that service interaction – happy music or doom and gloom?

What phrases could you use to help transition and assist that student, parent, or employer during an in-person interaction? Below are some great examples to use during a face-to-face interaction while using body language, facial expressions, and other nonverbals as support.

Service Excellence Examples:

- "That is a great question that I do not know the answer to, but I am going to find out the answer for us."

- "I would also be frustrated."

- "Please," "thank you," "you're welcome," "excuse me/pardon me."

- "We will keep you updated and let you know no later than (day/date/time)."

- "Yes," rather than "Yeah."

- "Thank you. We really appreciate you letting us know."

- "What I am going to do right now is…"

- "Will you?" rather than "You will."

- "Is there anything else I can help you with today?"

Consider This...

Be Careful of Inauthenticity

Phrases such as "You are a valued student" or "Your time is important to us" are likely true, but have a tendency to sound inauthentic when repeated in a script to a customer who is trying to get help resolving an issue. Instead of including empty reassurances in your script, show your customer how much they are valued by using polite tone and language and by demonstrating an understanding of the problem and any potential solutions.

In-Person Closings

Be sure to thank people for stopping in or for coming in personally, validating their choice to use their feet rather than a phone or email. Remind them of your services, upcoming events, or deadlines that would serve them well in the future and offer future service.

In-Person Closing Service Excellence Examples:

- "Thank you for stopping in; hope to see you back for our FYE Big Read Discussion next week."

- "Have/make it a great day!"

- "It was nice meeting you. Stop in any time."

What is NOT Service Excellence?

- "Sorry you had to deal with all of that; this place is horrible."

- "Uh-huh."

- (Head nod)

- Proceed to eat food and talk on personal phone call.

Final Thoughts

Scripting provides quality and consistent levels of service for customers and can easily be used within higher education. A pre-written conversation can provide a confidence and comfort level for the employees in various departments such as the Office for Admissions, University Recreation, and others. There are certain policy intensive areas within higher education in which we can use scripting to our benefit to better explain and communicate what otherwise might be more difficult.

Areas where scripting can assist in providing service excellence:

- Telephone service interactions (e.g, greetings, voice mail, explanations, apologies, and closings)

- Email communication skills

- In-person service moments (e.g., greetings, assisting with a difficult situation, and closings)

We must realize that customers can tell when a script is being used, but as long as we use the script as a guide and allow for personal interaction and improvisation, the customer is more likely to be satisfied with the experience. Script examples and exercises have been provided within this chapter, and we hope these tools are used and become a growing resource to improve your service delivery.

SECTION 5: CREATING ENVIRONMENTS THAT FACILITATE CUSTOMER SERVICE

Lead author for this chapter: Emily Richardson.

The way physical environments serve the customer is a key component to any customer service strategy, and yet you can probably think of at least one instance where the physical conditions in a service-oriented setting were less than appealing to you as the customer. Or, more importantly, you might have felt as if the physical design of a space did not meet your expectations.

Many institutions of higher education have old buildings, especially those institutions that began prior to 1900. We are proud of our heritage, but the fact remains that many campus buildings were designed and built long before the complexity of programs, administration, legal require-ments, and customer service concepts were even considered. Instead of thinking about the needs of the customer, we maintain our settings as if we were doing the work in the early 1900's. Personally, I was astonished when I found an old fashioned bank teller window with a megaphone still being used in the bursar's office in 2014!

Using a "Servicescape Audit" (co-developed by Academic Impressions and John Lehman, Associate Vice President for Enrollment and University Relations at Michigan Tech) as a guide, this chapter will introduce you to eighteen attributes that must be considered when designing customer-friendly physical space in higher education today. The audit will walk you through a process that you can follow to evaluate the Servicescape in your own area. In addition, two case studies which address the technology component of physical space will also be reviewed.

Conducting a Servicescape Audit

Before You Begin Your Audit

Before visiting any space on campus, you should ask and answer the following set of questions. If you can't fully answer them, then meet with the faculty or staff that utilize the space to get their ideas about the purpose of the space. These questions are to gain the basic information so that when the space is visited, the focus can be on how the space is accommodating the needs of the customer.

1. What function does this space have?

2. What do your customers need to be able to accomplish in this space?

3. Which customers use this space?

4. What times are customers in the space?

5. What physical/environmental attributes are necessary for customers to accomplish this?

6. Are items such as desks and chairs critical to the functionality of the space?

7. What types of technology are necessary for customers to access in this space?

8. What type of other implements (e.g., pens, paper, and staplers) might customers need access to in the space?

9. How do you want customers to feel while they are in this space?

10. Is this a quiet space or one where noise is welcomed?

11. Do you want the customers to be in a calming atmosphere, where the problems they are seeking to rectify don't seem so big?

12. What do you want this space to convey about your institution?

13. Do you want the customer to know from the signage and branding that they are welcome at the university?"

14. Are school colors critical for this space?

15. What do the customers currently say about the space?

16. Do they ever complain about the temperature?

17. Do they spend only the time they need to there? Do they rarely act as if they feel at home in the space?

18. Are students asking for more out of the space? What exactly are they asking?

Considerations When Visiting the Space

After these questions have been answered, it is critical to visit the space—and the visit is truly the key to the audit.

Go during peak business hours to get the truest sense of what the space is like. While responding to the questions asked in the audit, try to observe the space critically and through the eyes of a visitor. Take photos with your phone or digital camera to document how customers are interacting with the space, as well as what you perceive about different aspects of the space. It is important to write down your initial reactions to the space as well, specifically referencing the senses to describe that impression: What do you see? What do you hear? What do you smell? What do you feel?

To help you conduct a detailed audit, here are some more specific attributes you can think about while observing and experiencing different spaces on your campus:

QUESTIONS TO CONSIDER DURING YOUR AUDIT	
1. Organization	Is the space organized and free of clutter? What would the customer think about the organization of the space? Would they be able to find the information they are looking for? <u>Example</u> Can you imagine walking into a registrar's office where all you see are piles of papers? Would the student think that their request is simply going to be "added to the pile," or that it will be completed in a timely manner?
2. Cleanliness	Is the space clear? Are there adequate trash cans or other receptacles to help keep the space clean? If appropriate, is there a dispenser for hand sanitizer available to the customer? <u>Example</u> I'm a student who isn't feeling well, and I visit the health center on campus. When I arrive, I see a tiny trash can overflowing with used Kleenex. Am I going to believe that I'll be sicker after visiting the center, or that this is a place that understands my personal health?

3. Traffic flow	Are traffic patterns for customers moving within the space intuitive and clearly defined? Is it easy to tell where the line starts and ends? <u>Example</u> During the first week of classes, it is not unusual for dozens of students and parents to visit the bookstore on campus to procure their books. When it comes time to pay, is there a defined line? Can the customer tell how many individuals are in line ahead of them?
4. Quantity of Signage	Is there sufficient signage in the space to point customers in the right direction? <u>Example</u> Imagine going to an event on a college campus for the first time. Do you know where to park? Is there sufficient signage to help you find your way through the maze of a college campus?
5. Quality of Signage	Is existing signage legible, accurate, and positive?

	Example This sign is unclear and demanding in its tone. Is anyone paying attention to the signage used throughout the campus? TABLES ARE FOR EATING CUSTOMERS ONLY NO LOITERING
6. Volume Level	Is the noise level within the space (e.g., music, conversation, and other background noise) appropriate? Example We all appreciate the different kinds of music that are available, but can you remember being in a location where the music was so loud, you couldn't think or talk to another person without shouting? Sometimes rugs need to be placed in open spaces to help muffle sound and provide a quieter place.
7. Smells	Are the smells in the space appealing/appropriate for its function?

	Example
	At one point, the library on a college campus had a "no food" policy. But the staff room in the library had a microwave which was used every afternoon to cook popcorn! Guess what the students then smelled each afternoon, when they were not allowed food? That wonderfully strong scent of buttered popcorn.
8. Brightness/ Dimness of lighting	Is the space appropriately lit for its function? Example Imagine the alumni returning to campus to see the beautification projects that have occurred during the past 5 years. You take them into the admissions office, but due to the lighting and their poor eyesight, they can't read the signs or see the displays. Is there enough light, or too much light for the customers to see the fine print? If lighting is wrong, the customer will assume we are hiding something.
9. Quantity of furniture	Is there an appropriate amount of furniture in the space for what customers need to accomplish? What do the customers need to complete their work in the space? A table with seating? A standing table with writing elements? A collaborative work space with a white board?

	Example How many receptions (on and off of a college campus) have you been to where there just wasn't enough seating? Aesthetically, someone decided that the space would look better, based on the number of people attending, with fewer chairs and tables. And yet, the decision-makers in this situation aren't the ones standing with no place to put down a glass of wine or a plate of food. Having the right amount of furniture matters in every space.
10. Quality of furniture	Is the furniture in the space comfortable and in good condition? Example Have you ever sat in a chair that wasn't comfortable? If you sit in an uncomfortable chair, do you stay in that space long? It is critical that every piece of furniture is measured against its usability for the customer—not just whether it is right for the budget or for the aesthetics.
11. Décor	Is the décor appropriate for the space? Does it enhance the overall customer experience?

	Example I think this picture says it all!  I can remember when these first were designed and they seemed to end up on every desk. What message does that convey to the student, the customer, who is sitting there looking for answers?
12. Branding	Are there an adequate number of branded elements (i.e. colors, literature, etc.) to convey that this space is part of our institution? Example Does your admissions office look like every other admissions office – or can you tell the brand of your campus when you walk in? Multiple times, I've worked in offsite campus locations, and without the right signage they looked like any other corporate business. Adding colors, logos, or even a rug with the university seal in the entrance can make a big difference.

13. Employee Appearance	Is employee appearance (e.g., uniform, nametags, and a polished appearance) appropriate for the function of the space? Example Most hotels and restaurants have some sort of dress code for their employees so that you know who works for the company. In higher education, however, our front desks are often manned by work study students or by temporary employees during busy periods of time. Do they have a nametag on? Do they have the kind of appearance that "screams" professional, or are they dressed to go to class? Remember, your frontline employees greet your customers first. Sure, your customers usually enjoy meeting a student worker, but what does it say about your operation if they can't tell a student employee from a prospective student?
14. Quantity of Employees	Does the number of employees present appear to be proportional to or sufficient for the volume of customer traffic? Example We have all been in line at the grocery store, the statewide driver's license office, the store, or the bank when the line seems to be long. Usually, we are okay with waiting for a little bit, as long as we continue advancing in line and don't see someone "go off shift" for a break or lunch during the wait. This same principle applies to higher education as well.

	How can you plan better to manage volume during peak times?
15. ADA Compliance	Is the space ADA compliant? Example During my own 12-week stint in a wheelchair several years ago, I continuously encountered a small lip on the entrance to the bathroom that was almost impossible to maneuver with the wheelchair. It was deemed ADA compliant, but without help, it truly wasn't. Try to view your space from the vantage point of those who are blind, deaf, or have physical impairments. Make sure you have adequately prepared the space and educated your customer service representatives to assist them.
16. FERPA/ HIPAA Compliance	Does the physical design of the space take FERPA/HIPAA compliance into account? Example At one institution, a new advisor was suddenly needed on staff, but the room had been built originally as a closet, not as an office, and thus didn't have the same type of insulation as other offices. The institution decided that the only solution was to install a white noise machine to help sound-proof the area and safeguard against others overhearing when personal information was shared or discussed.

17. Cultural Sensitivity	Does the space appear to be designed in a way that is culturally sensitive? Would all types of students and customers feel comfortable in this space? Example International students are part of the university study body and they vary as to their ethnicity, religion, culture norms, and perception of America and its people. Yet, they have chosen to be in the US for their studies. We need to be sure that we take their backgrounds into consideration in terms of decorating. A simple example might be the placement of holiday decorations that are culturally diverse instead of specific Christmas decorations that, at many institutions, might be seen as less than culturally appropriate.
18. Welcoming	Overall, is this space welcoming? Example Have you ever wondered whether an office is open on a campus or closed? Is there a sign that says "Open" or "Closed," or that indicates its hours? We've all stood outside of a retail store or bank waiting for it to open at 9:00 a.m., when we obviously see activity inside. How is that scenario handled on your campus? What does it convey to the customer?

> Worse yet is the sign saying you are open until 5:30 p.m., and the door is locked at 4:30 p.m., with all of the lights off!

After Conducting the Audit

Once you have reviewed these 18 attributes, you then need to think about the customer and whether you feel they would be able to successfully accomplish what they need to in the space you have reviewed. If the answer is no, then what changes need to occur to enable them to experience a better level of customer service? Think about this in terms of both the makeup of the physical space and the actual items in the room, as well as the tone or the feeling that the space elicits.

Although an audit of this nature takes time, environmental considerations are a key component to customer service. Let's take a look at **two case studies** of physical space changes that occurred at institutions in response to this kind of thinking.

Case Study #1: RIT and the Campus Customer Information Desk

The Rochester Institute of Technology (RIT) in Rochester, New York was looking for a place where information could be provided to anyone on campus. In order to develop such a space, they needed to understand the competencies that the service staff would need to possess in order to properly serve customers. They began with an environmental scan, thinking about the space they currently had. They also thought about the customers and what they needed.

Here are some of the physical attributes of the space that the staff found to be barriers to service after conducting the environmental scan:

- A "garage door" style service window, circa 1965, complete with a sliding door that could be raised and lowered at will.

- A high desk with a recessed computer so that when customers approached, they were greeted by the top of the desk attendant's head, not a smiling face.

- A separate area in the back of the space where customers could make campus room reservations. Why was this area obscured? In case customers became dissatisfied and expressed concern it would happen privately.

The RIT staff decided to redesign the space to be approachable so that everyone—not just students, but families, visitors, and employees—would feel comfortable coming to reserve room space, find offices, get directions around campus, and generally seek information about everything that was happening on campus.

The space they eventually came up with was completely transformed. The area now feels welcoming and less restrictive, and is branded with the RIT logo and colors. The height of the desk was lowered so that the workers can look directly at the customer without computer monitors in the way. The front line employees can now see who is approaching the desk. The work study students wear school-colored jackets to help them look and feel more professional. The floor has a rug that features the Tiger mascot of RIT. It is also equipped with "interpretype" technology so that deaf and hard of hearing customers can communicate with desk workers. Most importantly, the space is welcoming to all!

Case Study #2: Widener University's One Stop

Widener University in Pennsylvania had a building on the edge of campus that housed the registrar's office, the bursar, and student financial aid offices. The difficulty with was that students entered one side of the building for the registrar's office, but then would have to go back out the door and around the building to the other side to get into the bursar and student financial aid offices.

To solve this problem, the administration decided to build a one-stop shop with ONE entrance to the building. Once it was complete, the students were greeted by a grouping of front line employees who were trained to help them with all their questions regardless of whether they were related to registration, billing, or financial aid.

Cross training was provided to all employees, along with thorough customer service training on how to effectively assist customers even when they were upset or unhappy. The main office felt welcoming and inviting, and there were smaller offices easily at hand for conversations that required confidentiality.

Final Thoughts

Creating the right environment for customer service is important and is often overlooked. As a leader, you must be aware of settings and conditions under which work occurs in any given space, and ensure that the space does not hamper good customer service. Often the process may be a result of the location of offices, which should be taken into account. In addition, the role of technology to solve customer problems must be considered. Technology is not always the answer, and poorly designed technology can often cause more problems, so planning in this area must be done carefully. Providing FAQ pages on commonly asked questions is one of the easiest ways to shrink the amount of phone calls in any customer-focused office. (For more on effective use of FAQs, see Section 2).

Take a close look at your physical environment using the **Servicescape Audit**. Then, evaluate the work processes you have to help your employees create the right types of environments that are conducive to providing good customer service.

SECTION 6: POLICIES AND PRACTICES THAT IMPACT SERVICE

Lead author for this chapter: Heath Boice-Pardee.

Federal, state, local, and university policies and practices may have a great impact on the service that you are able to provide to your customers. Understanding this impact will assist you in identifying how to mitigate challenges and enhance service.

By "policy," we mean the rule, and by "practice" we mean *how the rule is implemented.* For example, a policy might state that all emails are to be returned within 24 hours. As such, the practice would be to train staff to work within the 24 timeline and make reasonable efforts to follow the guideline (knowing that there may be exceptions).

Policies and practices that impact service might include:

- Those that are created and mandated for you (e.g., federal, state, etc.).

- Those your institution creates/maintains. (You may or may not have input or control over development and implementation.)

- Those that *you* develop. (Here, you have great investment and control.)

The government-initiated policies are the least flexible and often come with mandates that have great institutional impact if not precisely followed. For example, failure to adhere to federal guidelines such as discrimination policies can result in a loss of federal funds for the university and its students.

Many *institutional* policies/practices are also often fairly inflexible, but the consequences for not following them are not as dire for the institution. For example, there isn't much flexibility in the "add/drop" period for student registration, but failure to abide by this policy mostly impacts the customer (students). In this instance, most schools have the ability for students to withdraw from a course long after the add/drop period has passed. Finally, you have the most control over the policies and practices that you develop, but you may also have a personal bias that impacts your ability to assess and change them if necessary. In cases such as these, beware of continuing policies because "we've always done things this way," or continuing practices that were originally developed for a few "bad" customers.

First, determine whether you have any ability to control or change how the policy or practice is implemented. If there isn't anything you can do to change a policy, your time and energies are better spent elsewhere, such as considering your existing practice.

Evaluating Your Existing Policies and Procedures

Exercise!

Take a moment alone or with your team to identify and discuss policies and practices that have inhibited optimal customer service in your area:

- How can you make these policies or practices more customer-friendly?

- Can some of these practices be eliminated?

WORKSHEET: AUDITING POLICIES & PRACTICES

Consider some of the policies, procedures, or office "rules" that have been implemented. You can probably think of at least ten policies involved with recent service issues. List a few of those policies below:

1.

2.

3.

4.

5.

For the purpose of this exercise, don't focus on *why* the rule was put in place (even if you know), but consider *what* the impact is on your customers. This may help you to assess whether the policy or procedure is fine or needs tweaking. Then, you can create an action plan.

Example:

Policy/procedure: Office closes at 4:30 p.m.

What is the impact on our customers? Evening students cannot avail themselves of our services. We often miss calls from offices who are open later.

Action plan: Pilot later office hours until 6:00 p.m. 3 days per week to assess the traffic flow.

Now try a few for your office:

1. Policy/procedure: _____

_____

_____

_____

What is the impact on our customers? _____

_____

_____

_____

What is our action plan? _____

_____

_____

_____

_____

WORKSHEET, CONTINUED

2. Policy/procedure: _____

_____

_____

_____

What is the impact on our customers? _____

_____

_____

_____

What is our action plan? _____

_____

_____

_____

_____

3. Policy/procedure: _____

_____

_____

_____

What is the impact on our customers? _____

_____

_____

_____

What is our action plan? _____

_____

_____

_____

_____

Identify Choke Points

With more complex processes and procedures, one way to start defining both the impact a particular practice has on customers and the steps needed to remedy or improve it is to ask these questions:

- What is the most frequently asked question or complaint we hear from customers about this policy or procedure?

- What is one step we could eliminate?

- Who do I need to talk to, in order to get this done?

In particular, search for "choke points" that inhibit the delivery of optimal service. Most offices have them. These choke points can be physical boundaries where lines form, processes that stop the flow of service, or other barriers. You may already know about some of these choke points but haven't had an opportunity to fully consider a solution, or some of these service impediments may be new.

In order to identify and understand the choke points in your procedures and practices, consider a service that your office provides and put yourself in the role of the customer. Follow the process and service experience from start to finish. It will be best if you put yourself in the position of customer and walk through the process yourself.

The following "secret shopper" exercise may help you and your staff to identify these choke points and begin brainstorming solutions to mitigate them.

"SECRET SHOPPER" EXERCISE 1

Roleplaying a student or other customer, call your main office number.

What did you experience? _____

_____

_____

Were you greeted by a person or an automated message? _____

What was the greeting you received? _____

_____

_____

How many rings did it take before the phone was answered? _____

If you spoke to someone, were you told when you would receive a response? _____

Now that you've experienced the service:

How do you feel? _____

_____

Are there choke points? _____

_____

What can be improved? _____

_____

_____

_____

SECRET SHOPPER EXERCISE 2

We go to our office every day and often become oblivious to how our office spaces, especially our reception areas, look and feel to customers.

Ask a colleague who doesn't work in your office area everyday to visit, as though it's the first time. They should experience your space, services, etc. as a customer. After the visit, they might offer feedback on the following:

1. Upon entering the office, the first thing I noticed was: _____

_____

_____

_____

2. One aspect of the office that facilitates services is:

_____

_____

_____

_____

3. One aspect of the office that is a barrier to service is (consider placement of computer screen, desk placement, wall units, etc.) _____

_____

_____

_____

_____

4. This office makes me feel: _____

_____

_____

_____

_____

Now consider repeating the "Secret Shopper" exercise, again roleplaying a customer or inviting a colleague who is not as familiar with your office to roleplay a customer. This time, use the exercise to investigate:

- **Lines**.

  How do they form? Where do they form? Why do they form? What is causing the bottleneck? What can be improved?

- **Process time.**

  How long does it take the office to process material? What is the impact on the customer? How can this be streamlined or better communicated to the customer?

Developing New Policies and Procedures

When considering the creation of a new policy or practice, it is important to ask yourself and others in your department these questions:

- How will this new policy or practice positively impact customer service?

- How does this new policy or practice relate to our service competencies?

- What policies and practices currently exist?

Starting with these questions will help you and your team determine how to proceed to devise policies and practices that serve customers in positive ways.

Considering the Impact on Service

It is vital to consider the potential impact on customer service. Some considerations include:

- Impact to information access.

- Ability to reach a mutually beneficial agreement.

- Ability to show concern/care.

- Impact on security/safety.

- Alignment with institutional values.

- Alignment with institutional priorities.

Impact on Information Access

There is certainly information that must be kept confidential, but communication transparency is key to maintaining positive customer interactions. If you must develop a policy or practice that limits information sharing, it is best to communicate this broadly before a request (or demand) happens. It is also crucial to share your reason for not sharing information. For example, in the United States, employees at colleges and universities are bound by FERPA (Family Education Rights and Privacy Act) which guides what information can be shared about students. FERPA is not likely to change as a policy (and would require the government to make a change). However, the way employees work within FERPA (practices) may be considered.

An existing practice regarding FERPA might be to simply explain that federal law prohibits you from sharing information about students. Simply stating, "I'm sorry, I can't share that information," to an upset parent will only heighten the frustration. While this is accurate, it is not likely very satisfying to a parent seeking information about their daughter or son. A better practice might be in order. It will be much better to say, "I understand that this is a concern, and I will be happy to share that information with you as long as I get permission from your daughter (student). I can't legally share the information you are requesting without written consent." While this may not make the parent happy, it does explain your reasons in a transparent way.

Consider This...

What CAN You Say?

Instead of stating that you cannot divulge information based on law, you might practice speaking in generalities. An example of this could be, "While I can't speak specifically about your son's conduct case, I can share that in cases similar to what you are describing, students are not typically suspended from the university." Another option is to reassure the parent that with their child's consent, you are happy to speak freely.

Ability to Reach a Mutually Beneficial Agreement

While it is great when we can make customers happy, it is also nice when we can find common ground that is agreeable to the department as well. For example, although students may want to utilize your services beyond 5:00 p.m., this may not be a staffing possibility. Identifying one or two days where after-hours appointments can be arranged will make your students (customers) happy, while also putting your department and team in a positive light.

Consider This...

Is Rigidity Impacting Customer Service?

While policies and practices are critical to managing daily operations, they should always be executed with thought. One size cannot fit all. For example, some faculty have "mandatory attendance" policies. While the spirit of this policy is understandable, it's not always reasonable in practice. Emergencies happen, and policies must sometimes be bent to accommodate. During Hurricane Irma, Walt Disney World suspended its policy on pets and allowed guests to house their properly secured and managed pets safely in the resorts. This change helped guests with stranded pets, and likely didn't offer tremendous disruption to non-pet-lovers given the condition of the policy to keep pets secure.

Photo: From a friend of the author. Used with permission.

Showing Concern/Care

This is a great place to begin in developing any policy or practice. It is important to show that you care for the welfare of your customers and departmental staff. At the Marriott corporation, a core value is "Take care of associates and they will take care of the customers."

Showing your concern for those around you when developing new policies and practices humanizes this sometimes mundane process.

Impact on Security/Safety

Consider This...

Do Customers Understand Why?

Sometimes customer frustration comes from a lack of understanding. It is important to communicate a policy clearly and also to explain the motive behind it. Using Walt Disney World as an example, sometimes attractions are closed even after guests have waited in line for an hour or more. Sometimes the reason is mechanical, but often the reason is weather-related. Explaining that there is an impending thunder storm with lightning may not ease frustration, but it does offer an explanation that cannot be challenged.

Security and safety are paramount to customer ease and satisfaction. At the Walt Disney Company, the first company value is "safety." Thus, every policy and practice developed at Disney must consider how customer (guest) and staff (cast members') safety is impacted. Since this is readily communicated throughout the Disney company, this transparency fosters greater customer understanding and buy-in. For example, if a guest is asked to remove his/her backpack or hat prior to getting-on an attraction, knowing that this practice is rooted in the interest of safety (and not simple inconvenience) helps the customer understand the motive.

Alignment with Institutional Values and Priorities

When developing a new policy or practice it is important that it doesn't conflict with any overarching institutional value or priority. For example, if an institution's value is "students first," but you want to change your office hours to more easily accommodate staff, it is important to consider if there is a conflict. If there is, institutional values and priorities should always eclipse departmental desire/need.

Steps to Take

In order to develop a policy and practice, you may consider the following steps:

- **Identify the problem.**

   What is it that you are trying to solve or improve? Who will the policy or practice impact and at what cost? Will the policy or practice serve your customers and community well?

- **Write for clarity.**

   Consider your audience. A policy written for students might be written more conversationally than a policy for faculty. Have others read your draft and point out questions or inconsistencies that you may not have considered. Do a "walk-through." When the policy has been drafted, walk through how it will be implemented step by step. This will illuminate blind spots and challenges that need to be addressed before implementation.

- **Develop a communication plan.**

  How will you communicate the existence and
  rationale for your new policy? Consider your
  audience. Will an email suffice, do you need to do
  a "dog and pony show" at large staff meetings, or
  do you need an ad campaign? You will likely need
  a combination of strategies.

- **Measure your effectiveness.**

  After implementation, monitor the mood of
  customers and seek feedback. In order to gain
  feedback, you may consider speaking directly with
  constituents, sending out an email or paper survey,
  or identify some other way to capture the pulse
  around the issue.

Identifying, implementing, and constantly evaluating
policies and practices that impact your delivery of service
excellence is key to consistently satisfying customers.
While writing new policy is favored by few, doing so with
a strong rationale, motive to enhance service, and desire to
consistently monitor impact are key. Examining and
enhancing the implementation, adaptation, or creation of
policies and practices will enhance communication
between service providers and customers, allow for more
transparency, and amplify your ability to provide excellent
customer service.

Implementing Policies and Practices in Ways that Boost Service

Given the number of policies and practices by which colleges and universities must abide, staying up to date can seem daunting. The following are tips on how to understand and implement various policies and practices on-campus.

Federal and Local Policies and Practices

Depending on the country in which you live, there are a variety of governmental policies and practices that likely impact your work and service to customers. As discussed before, in the United States, FERPA (Family Educational Rights and Privacy Act) is well-established for limiting the types of student information that can be shared with others. In Canada, the Accessibility for Ontarians with Disabilities Act (AODA) addresses how universities must provide access to students. There are many others. These are the best ways to implement such policies on your campuses:

- **Enhance understanding and awareness.** Do what you can to educate your customers about the laws/policies and why you are responding accordingly.

- **Rely on campus experts.** You can't know every law or the specifics of every national guideline. Rely on campus experts who have studied these and rely on their expertise. University lawyers are great resources!

- **Provide training for staff and students.** Identify ways that you can educate and train the people who are charged with implementing the federal law, as well as your customers. This transparency can facilitate communication and dialogue.

- **Keep current.** Since laws can change, it is important to stay current on topics important to your office. Be sure to follow professional publications or listservs and share information with staff, students, and others as appropriate.

Consider This...

Keep Current

Since many national laws change frequently, consider "assigning" one or two individuals on your team to monitor and provide updates as needed. In the United States, Title IX (which governs sexual discrimination, assault, and harassment) guidelines have been subject to many changes recently. Designating a "go-to" person for updates avoids duplication of efforts and saves time.

SAMPLE POLICY/PROCEDURE WORKSHEET		
Policy/Procedure	**Resource**	**Go-To Person**
Example: RIT Policy D.18, Student Conduct Policy	Webpage for the student handbook	Director of Student Conduct or Office of Legal Affairs
FAFSA		
Title IX		
FERPA		
HIPAA		
(OTHER)		

Institutional Policies and Practices

There are many campus-specific policies and practices that impact your workflow and dealings with customers. Some examples include your university's class-registration process, financial aid deadlines, student conduct policies, and even restrictions on smoking. In order to implement such policies, keep these in mind:

- **Enhance understanding and awareness.**

  Determine how you can educate your departmental staff and customers on the reasons for policies, history, and benefits. This transparency can facilitate positive customer interactions.

- **Dig to understand the "why."**

  Oftentimes, departments engage in behaviors and activities out of habit. "Because we've always done it that way" is never the optimal response. If there is a confusion about how a policy or practice came to be, research the issue to find its history. Knowing the "why" can help others buy-in.

- **Rely on campus experts.**

  If you don't know why a policy or practice exists on your campus, find someone who does. Knowing this valuable history can help you make a decision on whether a policy or practice needs to be updated or laid to rest.

Office-Specific Policies and Practices

You may deal with departmental policies and practices more than any others. Your office might have rules regarding how to reserve space, how to best respond to email and phone calls, how to greet customers, and more.

Consider the following when working with such office-specific policies:

- **Strive for Consistency.**

  Are policies and practices in your department consistent with those across campus? You can always strive to be better, but make sure that your level of customer service is minimally on par with other campus areas. Look for ways in which you can excel in service delivery.

- **Avoid the historical trap.**

  "We've always done it this way" is a common reason for implementing a policy or practice on a daily basis. Continually assess the reason/need for such an office guideline and determine if it needs to be modified or removed.

Final Thoughts

Policies and practices can guide your office's ability to provide service excellence. Whether you develop your own policies and practices, or enhance your knowledge of resources to help guide you in following those created for you, understanding is critical. Remember that you don't need to be an expert on policies that you didn't create- you just need to identify your go-to resources to help you know how to respond to customers' questions. Enhancing your understanding will allow you and your team to provide consistent responses, which will lead to enhanced customer satisfaction.

SECTION 7: CULTIVATING FACULTY AND STAFF BUY-IN

Lead author for this chapter: Emily Richardson.

This chapter will discuss the resistance you may face from some campus partners, who may not immediately buy into the concept of enhancing customer service in higher education. We will offer strategies that can be used to gain the support of faculty and staff and invite their acceptance of a "customer friendly" strategy.

The model for this chapter will be based on Kouzes and Posner's five practices of exemplary leadership, as outlined in the book *The Leadership Challenge*. These practices include:

1. **Model the Way**

2. **Inspire a Shared Vision**

3. **Challenge the Process**

4. **Enable Others to Act**

5. **Encourage the Heart**

Whether you are a department head, supervisor, or a director or assistant director in higher education, you can make customer service a goal of your department. Or, if you are a vice chancellor, provost, or president who has the power to make customer service an institutional imperative. In either case, using the concepts for exemplary leadership to frame the conversation in your department or on campus is critical so that others understand the importance of the strategy—and also so that the results achieved are those desired.

1. Model the Way

This is a simple but powerful practice in that it will be your behavior that wins you respect and also sets the expectations for others. Your voice must be the one that demonstrates the importance of customer service both as the action of service and also as part of your core values. So think about the following questions and pay attention to your answers. They will help you understand the ideas behind modeling the way.

- When you greet a customer, are you standing or sitting?

- Do you use the customer's name in the conversation—not just once but multiple times?

- Do you practice active listening with the customer?

- When was the last time you expressed to your work group how important every customer is to the organization?

- When was the last time you asked your customers (both internal and external) what their expectations were? When was the last time you shared these expectations with your frontline staff?

- Is the word *customer* in the mission statement for the university or the department?

- Do you treat internal customers different than external customers?

If you can answer "yes" to these questions (which get at the core competencies of service), then you have already established customer service as a core value. If not, then you need to begin to practice the art of customer service every day, thereby demonstrating to everyone else the importance of customer service to you.

> "*Setting the Example* is all about execution. It's about putting your money where your mouth is. It's about practicing what you preach. It's about following through on commitments. It's about keeping promises. It's about walking the talk. It's about doing what you say. And because you're leading a group of people – not just leading yourself – it's also about what those who are following you are doing. How consistent are they in deed and word? How well are they practicing what's preached? As the leader, you're held accountable for their actions, too."
> (Kouzes and Posner, 76).

2. Inspire a Shared Vision

An exemplary leader defines the future for others. They articulate the vision, purpose, mission, and future aspirations of their department or the university through the words and stories that they tell. They also must be careful not to let those words be only those of the leader. A good leader will work with others to find a common purpose through a process of listening.

Faculty may well be the first to question a customer service initiative, especially if they do not have a voice at the table for the discussion. Yet I would propose that with dialogue, it should be possible to reach the following points of agreement regarding customer service in the classroom, in the community, and on the campus:

1. Interactions with others will be respectful and conducted with common courtesy.

2. The customer (internal and external) will be listened to for the purpose of understanding.

3. Interpersonal skills will be used to help to deescalate problems and resolve concerns.

4. Employees will be empowered to find creative solutions to aid in customer satisfaction—within the scope of their responsibilities.

5. The core values of respect for diversity and safety are imperative to customer service.

By no means is this an all-inclusive list, and it will vary based on whether your service initiative is department-specific or encompasses the entire university. In no way do any of these equate to the notion that the "student is always right"; instead, these concepts serve to assure and inspire everyone involved to create a community that operates on trust, respect, and shared values.

As a leader, you must also take this shared vision and place it into words. Disney, Ritz Carlton, and Tom's Shoes have all had leaders who spoke from the heart about their commitment to customers, and they were able to tell the story of the future in such a way that each employee could see themselves in that story and in the future of the company.

The Customer Isn't Always Right

When challenging the concept of students as "customers," some may use the argument, "The customer isn't always right. We're not Disney."

Consider This...

This is true—and in fact, Disney says "no" to customers all the time. It is important to say no with respect and to offer alternative solutions, if possible. Customers don't always need to be right, but they *do* always need to feel heard.

---

3. Challenge the Process

When beginning a customer service strategy, every leader must begin to challenge the current process in every area of campus. The leader must put the customer first and ask the question of "why" when reviewing processes and procedures. Even office placement can get in the way of serving a student who must cross a campus to have to resolve problems between financial aid, billing, and registration.

A leader must realize that small wins early on will set the stage for larger changes in the future. "Innovation requires more listening and communication than does routine work" (Kouzes and Posner, p. 177). Any change requires relationship building, communication, and proactive interaction with others to make a difference. Change for the customer will occur when the leader begins to actively listen to their employees and watch the process of service.

If you are looking for opportunities to be innovative, you need to be present in the place and time for the student. Here are two examples:

Move-in day

What is the line of cars like? Is there signage? What information was sent to the students prior to arrival? What was sent to the parents? Is there a bottleneck picking up keys? Are people having trouble finding help to move in refrigerators? This is the first day, a key day that sets the stage for the student at the university. So, can we make it even better? Is someone handing out free, cold water to parents and students during move-in? Are there ambassadors in some kind of recognizable attire, who are prepared to answer ANY question? Is the greeting for the day scripted? Does everyone have a positive, customer friendly attitude?

The first day of evening classes

As someone who has served the working adult, it never fails to amaze me how few offices are open on campus after 5:00 p.m. during the first week of classes.

Frequently, classes are moved, and no signage is
posted. Students arrive and can't find parking, and
there is no one to guide them. The financial aid office
and registrar's office are closed, and there is no one
there to offer them guidance on how to pay their bill
or change a class.

Are there schools that handle both of these problems in
innovative ways that satisfy the customer? Absolutely, but
the majority of schools are still doing things the way they
have always done them, without feedback from the
customer and without anyone thinking about how minor
changes might improve the customer service experience.

If you are unsure where to start, think about the
complaints that have come from students, parents, faculty,
and community members to leadership within the
university. If someone has written a complaint, odds are
high that there are others with the same complaint who
haven't taken the time to formally lodge it, and instead
have just not returned to your university. These complaints
are a great first place to look for wins—they may be small
wins, but they will be meaningful ones to your customers.

4. Enable Others to Act

This exemplary practice of leadership, enabling others to
act, is necessary for change to occur. Trust must be created
through relationship building so that each and every
department on campus that interacts with customers
understands the difficulties and problems that come with
their service. This is also critical within a given department.
Ask: Does each member of the team understand the
responsibilities of the other members?

Getting people to interact sounds simple and easy, and yet
in the world of the Internet and email, many higher

education institutions are becoming more about silos than interaction. When was the last time you, as a leader, managed by walking around? When was the last time you brought together individuals from a department that works with yours to iron out the problems you are facing together, in person? When was the last time you thanked others for the service they give to your customers?

At Queens University of Charlotte, our department instituted a cookie tray "thank you" at the holidays, where every member of the staff either purchased or made holiday cookies. We spent time as a group putting the trays together and wrote special notes to each department thanking them for serving our adult students. This was a simple gesture, but one that helped pave the way for ongoing conversations and discussions focused on changes for the adult students on campus.

In order to further develop trust, a leader must ensure that employees are held accountable for their actions, but must also provide opportunities for education and training to help employees effectively carry out the critical tasks they perform. Investing in customer service training for front-line employees will allow them to develop competence and confidence in their skills, thereby enabling them to provide better customer service on a day-to-day basis.

In addition, the leader must coach others to strengthen their abilities and confidence. It is critical that as a leader they understand that they are accountable for customer service. At the same time, a leader can empower the employees to make more decisions. For example, consider the number of signatures needed to make something happen for a student. Are all of these signatures really needed? What freedom does a frontline employee have to adjust the rules? Is there a way that routine work can be given to other employees during extremely busy times for front line staff?

5. Encourage the Heart

Not all leaders are good leaders, but those who are show their appreciation and celebrate with their team the contributions that each person brings to the success of a customer service-oriented culture. As a leader, you have the right to expect the best from each individual, but at the same time, this means you must personalize your recognition so that each individual feels valued and knows that you care.

For some employees, a simple "thank you" is all that is needed, while for others a handwritten thank you card would ensure that they will continue to give you their best moving forward. For some, it is a quiet moment in the leader's office with just the two talking about the contribution; for others, public recognition is what sings out to them. Do you know each employee well enough to identify what type of recognition they would appreciate? If you don't, you aren't spending enough time getting to know each individual. Some call it CBWA (Caring by Wandering About), others call it MBWA (Management by Walking Around). In either case, spending time with front line employees sends the message that you care about them, about customer service, and about the vision you passionately communicated to them.

Celebrating success allows you to reinforce core values of customer service, but it also allows you to tell the story of "Why" and "How" we satisfied a customer. Stories become a form of communication, and those stories are often the things that stick in team members' minds and compel them to carry them through an extra hard day. As a leader, you need to share your story – but also share the stories of your staff to leadership, so that they can see the difference of customer service values at work.

So what about the Faculty?

If you are a leader of faculty, can you convince them that students are customers? Or is this an argument not worth having? As stated earlier, it is about finding a common set of values. In the case of faculty, the strongest shared set of values is around student learning. An effective way to frame the conversation with faculty is: "How do we create a university where our students can focus on learning and development? In this case, what do we need to provide the student to ensure that their learning can be front and center? As a faculty member, what do you need to do to provide for student learning?"

The answers to these questions will vary to some degree, but at the same time, the answers really do focus on the student as a customer. You can also ask, "What is the student looking for from a faculty member?" Examples:

- *A complete syllabus* that includes learning outcomes, timelines, assignments, teaching philosophy, grading schema, and how to be successful in the course. This is a standard prerequisite to meeting the needs of the student.

- *A feedback mechanism that is well-explained and timely.* Regular feedback is something all students want, and yet some faculty feedback is not offered in any regular format. Studies demonstrate that regular feedback contributes to improved learning.

- *Timely responses to student questions.* These can be difficult to achieve in this 24/7 world of email. Faculty can set expectations by including on their syllabi that they will respond to questions within a 24- or 48-hour period. For non-assignment-specific questions, they can also provide an FAQ page based on previous emails and questions asked for student reference.

- *Office hours.* Either in person or virtually, these hours are important for many students. Students may not use them all the time, but they want to know that the faculty member is there. How are faculty members making sure that the office hours they present on their syllabus are "held for the student" throughout the entire semester?

- *Other ways to get to know faculty.* Office hours provide one such way, but others could include seeing faculty attend the athletic events, sitting in the stands with other students. Or the faculty could invite their students to meet for coffee at the campus coffee house at different times during the semester. Whatever the method, what counts is that students are getting the opportunity to see the faculty outside of the classroom. This helps students see that faculty do care about the entire student experience, whether curricular or co-curricular.

- *Knowing students' names.* Depending on the size of the campus, getting to know the students by name can be difficult. Yet, there is nothing better to be called by your name. Faculty need to work at learning their student's names and then using their names both in and out of the classroom.

Most faculty have not had a conversation about what part they play in the student experience, because the academic enterprise is at the center of their being. Yet, one wonders whether that conversation would add items to this list that could become the new standard for student expectations from faculty.

Final Thoughts

Leadership is not easy, and it becomes even harder when you are leading change in the culture. Customer service is also more difficult to lead because it is intangible.It is difficult to measure good customer service; without a discussion about values and key concepts, a leader will have a tough time seeing the change occur. Begin with the small wins: the places that you know can and should be changed, where the customer will start to see the change. Celebrate those wins. That will lead to the beginning of culture change towards excellence in customer service on campus.

SECTION 8: POST-SECONDARY EXAMPLES OF CUSTOMER SERVICE EXCELLENCE

Lead author for this chapter: Eileen Soisson.

This section will look at four best practices that have strongly contributed to the success of service excellence programs in higher education. We will also offer some guidance for replicating similar practices at your own institution. We will also provide supporting examples of these best practices through institutional profiles that highlight their service program—noting which of these best practices have contributed to that program's success and achievement of its goals.

What Enables Excellence in Customer Service

Institutions that provide models of excellence in customer service share common characteristics:

1. **Leadership support** for improvement and excellence in customer service—and clear ownership of the service excellence initiative.

2. **Support groups** (such as an advisory team, steering committee, or task force) to guide the initiative forward and build momentum.

3. **A customer service training** or professional development program.

4. **A recognition program** rewarding examples of excellent customer service on campus.

5. A **clear plan** for evaluating and measuring improvement in customer service.

Before we look at specific models at post-secondary institutions, let's take a closer look at each of these four items that need to be in place in order for such a model to be successful. Then, we will look at how various institutions put all four of these in place and saw real improvement.

1. Leadership

Someone has to own the initiative and communicate the vision, the why, and the benefits of a service excellence program for the university. In certain institutions, a service program is isolated to one area and that leader is the director; in others, the service program is university-wide with a designated point person/leader. Leadership is either going to run the program or appoint someone who will create, implement, and carry out the needed structure for the initiative. It is the leadership's or point person's responsibility to establish minimum standards and steps of service for the university. These standards help to set expectations and guide behaviors with current and future service interactions.

The university's leadership must cast the vision for a culture that moves toward a more defined, long-term "customer focus." The vision is communicated more effectively through constant repetition and the message that the program is not "just another knee-jerk decision administration is going to try for six months."

The vision must be clear. For the most part, people must want to be part of the energy that exists to make the university better. The vision must set clear expectations of what service looks like at your university and how that is different than anywhere else. Create an energy that is contagious (pardon the cliché), and employees are much more likely to get on board.

As Jim Collins states in *Good to Great*, the aspiration is to have the people on the figurative bus headed in the same direction. "It is better to first get the right people on the bus, the wrong people off the bus, and the right people in the right seats, and then figure out where to drive" (p. 41). If leadership can effectively communicate the vision, the why, and the benefits to the movers and shakers, momentum is more likely. It is important to capture and celebrate that along the way. Retention applies to keeping those customers (external *and* internal) that will steer the university bus in the right direction toward the service vision of the institution.

With all eyes on the leader, the leadership of the institution must demonstrate the standard of customer service performance to be emulated by all faculty and staff through personal example. "The first person who has to deliver excellent service to everyone is the president. If he or she is not capable of making people feel as if they matter and are valued at the very least, that sets a tone that pervades the entire institution" (Raisman, p. 8).

2. Support Groups: Advisory Team, Steering Committees, Task Force

Especially in the early stages of a service program implementation, "building an army" is vital to move the message and momentum forward. This group should be formed around its purpose and desired outcomes. If an initiative is in its early stages, an advisory team or steering committee might serve best. This group would help guide the initiative through constant feedback, assessment, and "think tank" style sessions. Ideal members of this committee will include representatives from faculty, staff, housing, campus recreation, admissions, and any other service-strong departments.

Committee members should communicate frequently by way of email, telephone, committee meetings, and personal visits to ensure timely flow of ideas. The focus of the meetings will be to review progress and to address concerns and challenges that may hinder the implement-ation of a process, alter/threaten the friendliness of the team, and/or make things easier.

A task force would support leadership and the initiative by focusing on specific goals or projects within a particular time. For example, a task force may have the charge of creating an initial assessment of strengths, weaknesses, opportunities, and threats in regard to university-wide service and then reporting the results to the leadership team, advisory group, etc. Task force groups can also assume responsibility for specific areas such as marketing, quality control, student training, etc.

3. Customer Service Training or Professional Development Program

"If they haven't caught it, then we haven't taught it."

Training is key to setting the necessary expectations of the service culture you are trying to change, enhance, or create for your institution. To better serve students, Ewers suggested that institutions have employees attend customer service training sessions to learn the basics of customer service, yet many in academia find this a hard pill to swallow. But by providing the needed instruction and expectation level of university service skills, this creates a universal understanding and sets everyone up for more success.

Training Programs

Many universities have a basic training course created to cover the basics of service and what that means specifically for their university. Other institutions have created a training program built of several training sessions with certification upon successful completion. The trainings vary, but they all cover what appears to be most important for customer satisfaction within their area/campus. Some trainings focus on the new values or standards while others may focus on the new service skills, competencies, and behaviors that are to be implemented into daily interactions.

Training should be created specific for that particular institution. A program is more likely to sustain if it is true to the fabric of the institution and not simply copied from somewhere else. Participants will know the training is authentic if it resonates with the culture and the hope of a stronger community.

A strong recommendation is to pilot the training program within a service-focused area such as university recreation, housing, student accounts, etc. Present the first training, test out the content, record attendance while figuring out that logistic, analyze feedback, and make improvements before launching it to another department or institution as a whole. This type of departmental training will allow trainers/facilitators the opportunity to glean current day examples and use them for future trainings.

Content and examples are best to be higher-education specific. Avoid using Disney and Ritz-Carlton as the only examples; instead, spotlight other universities and their successes. If you are in the early stages of creating a training program and want to implement something used from a hospitality background, be sure to make it relevant and applicable to higher education. It is best not to try to convert your campus with an initial Disney approach, because it is truly like comparing apples to oranges, as shared earlier in this book.

Training sessions and professional development work-shops focused on service will have benefits and will hopefully be reflected in future retention scores. "Following a workshop at the University of Maine in Fort Kent, retention was reported to have increased 5% by UMFK Provost Dr. Rachel Albert. This was 2% more than the administration had hoped for and was achieved because the University took the ideas from the workshop and made them part of the culture" (Raisman, p. 14).

A strong suggestion is to think twice about making it mandatory. That word automatically creates an association to the compliance trainings we are expected to take annually within higher education, such as sexual harass-ment, general safety, protection of minors, etc. An alternative approach that appears to work is using the term "strongly encourage" and create every opportunity for early supporters to take part in the training. Offer sessions at 7:00 a.m. for the facilities grounds crew to accommodate their work schedule; present a customer service training session at departmental retreats; and make sure that those who have embraced the training and its values are rewarded and recognized. A goal is to create a culture of "get to" versus "got to" when introducing the training program.

Train the Trainer Program

Are you wondering now how you are going to train everyone in your department, college, or university? A "train the trainer" program involves training employees from other offices to lead customer service training or provide open sessions for their own department. Those trainers have the same passion, knowledge, and support for the program. Some colleges select those individuals through an application, nomination, or volunteer process. This allows for customer training to be a more consistent and constant process and not just an annual event, while also ensuring an adherence to the brand within everyday service.

New Employee Orientation

Ideally, all newly hired employees at a university would complete a formal orientation program that includes an overview of the university's commitment to customer service. The most opportune time to introduce employees to the service program is at new employee orientation, so don't miss this chance to share the expectations early. A simple overview of the program, service expectations, and training opportunities should be covered.

4. Recognition Program

"Catch people doing things right" is a key lesson behind Ken Blanchard's *One Minute Manager*. The more ways we can catch and celebrate people doing service things right, the more likely we can positively reinforce that behavior and the overall culture on campus.

A culture of service should include an environment that encourages and rewards employees who take ownership of customer issues and who use their initiative to address customer concerns in a timely and efficient manner. To this end, an employee recognition program (one based on established criteria to celebrate and reward individual employees and service teams who provide superior support to the customers) is key to include in the early stages of implementation. Connect the criteria of the recognition program to the values. Reward what you want to see more of within your institution. We will share examples of service recognition programs within the institutional profiles at the end of this chapter.

Consider This...

Naming Your Recognition Program

Name the recognition program something that is connected to your school's colors, mascot, tagline, etc. This ties the program to the university's brand.

5. Evaluation and Measurement

"You can't expect what you don't inspect."

Colleges and universities who have started a service program realize the importance of evaluating the program and seeking ways to tie service to retention—but that is easier said than done. We can evaluate the programs created, rate the responsiveness to the trainings, and review the comment cards of praise for exceptional care for a student, but no one has figured out the magical equation of how to tie all of this back to retention. This is the million-dollar question: How do you measure the impact of service excellence on retention?

Methods of evaluating performance improvement include, but are not limited to: web-based surveys, comment cards, training workshop evaluations, on-the-spot comments through campus interviews, personal oral or written testimonials, and—eventually—retention as a customer service indicator.

Consider:

- Quality assurance audits

- Servicescape audit

- Secret shopping or mystery shopper program

- Focus groups of students/customers

- Pre-/post assessments in auxiliary service areas such as housing

- Exit interviews

- Mapping (A tool that can be used to review each step of a process/service through the eyes of the customer and determine areas of opportunity at each step to provide excellent customer service)

- Institutional performance appraisal should include customer service as a primary rating area for enhanced departmental and personal account-tability. Employees supporting the initiative through attitude and action should be recognized and rewarded. Supervisors of any employees demonstrating deficiencies in this area should develop individual improvement plans to assist the employees in enhancing their performance.

Note that the best survey results or focus group findings are those that are acted on, debriefed, and disseminated to appropriate faculty and staff and communicated in effective ways.

Consider This...

Conduct a Customer Service Survey

The institutional research department at your university can mostly likely create, administer, and compile the survey results to gather feedback from students, employees, and external cust-omers regarding the consistency and usefulness of information received, timeliness of assistance, and the level of customer service received. These survey results may create additional action items to work toward to achieve exceptional and friendly customer service.

Profiles of Customer Service Excellence at Colleges and Universities

Let's look at six institutions (listed in alphabetical order) that are implementing a customer service program on their campus and identify any best practices to advance service efforts and goals.

Central Michigan University

Mount Pleasant, Michigan
Public institution
26,080 undergraduate students

Central Michigan University offers more than 200 undergraduate degree programs and more than 70 graduate degree programs. These programs are in areas ranging from the health professions and educational leadership to business and information systems. There are 2,600 faculty and staff.

CMU's service excellence program began in 2001 to enhance employees' professional skills in a wide range of learning opportunities. Service values of CMU faculty and staff are care, knowledge, availability, and follow-through.

Leadership or Advisory Group

The Leadership Standards Initiative falls under the Office of the President. The Service Excellence Initiative is led by the Service Excellence Advocates Committee, and there are currently nine members representing various areas of the institution (e.g., Human Resources, University Communications, Student Success, Residence Life, Information Technology, etc.)

Training or Professional Development Program

The program had a 15th Anniversary Service Excellence Celebration in October 2016. After this event, "a list of service value behaviors was compiled based on suggestions from those in attendance." This list is available online as a training and development resource. Other service resources available for employees include quizzes, a survey, fire-up tips of the week, and information on facilitating service excellence discussions with staff.

Service Excellence Open Workshops include a general overview of service, how to keep the vision alive and working with difficult customers. Service Excellence Department Workshops are delivered to specific departments by request, and they provide general overviews of service and the University's Service Excellence Initiative. The department workshops can be highly customized to meet departmental needs. The workshops are delivered by Professional Development Programs (PDP).

Lee Cockerell (former executive vice president of operations at Walt Disney World) spoke with the employees and gave presentations (Leadership and Customer Service; Leadership/Management) at CMU in October 2016. These sessions were recorded and can be found online as a resource for university employees. Faculty and staff showed support with this program through 20 groups sponsoring Cockerell's appearance.

Service Excellence Stories

Excellent examples of customer service happen on campus everyday. Read and share your experiences with us.

View Stories

Person or Department you're nominating or a Title for this story:*

Your First Name:*

Your Last Name:*

Email

Phone Number

Your Story * (2000 Character Limit)

☐ I agree the service excellence advocates reserves the right to approve, edit, or decline any submissions, and that information provided is accurate and factual.

Submit Your Story   Cancel

Recognition Method

CMU reinforces its service values of care, knowledge, availability, and follow-through by recognizing outstanding staff who routinely and regularly demonstrate commitment to and support of said values. CMU's Staff Excellence Award Program is designed to recognize and reward individuals in the service-maintenance (e.g., facilities, dining, and storeroom/warehouse), professional and administrative, office professional, public broadcasting, police, sergeants, and supervisory-technical employee groups. Winners of the Staff Excellence Award Program are announced each August. Winners receive a plaque, a one-year pre-paid parking pass, and recognition at the annual Staff Excellence Award Program Ceremony.

CMU shares their service excellence stories on their webpage (see page 170), which is a great way to celebrate the excellent examples of customer service that happens on their campus every day. Employees, visitors, and students can submit a story and the site will also share the submitted stories highlighting the various service superstars.

For more information about Central Michigan's service excellence program, visit:

https://www.cmich.edu/fas/hr/serviceexcellence/Pages/default.aspx.

Coastal Carolina University

Conway, South Carolina
Public institution
10,400 undergraduate students

CCU offers 73 areas of study toward the baccalaureate degree and 21 graduate level programs. The graduate level programs include 18 master's degrees, including those in education, writing, coastal marine and wetland studies, and the MBA; two educational specialist degrees; and two Ph.D. degrees, one in marine science and the other in Education.

There are approximately 468 full-time faculty and 730 full-time staff.

Leadership or Advisory Group

The Feel the Teal® Initiative was launched by the Office of the President in summer 2011. President David A. DeCenzo appointed a leadership team made up of university leaders and then appointed a director of Service Excellence (Eileen Soisson) to oversee the implementation. After five years, the leadership team served its initial purpose to oversee the execution of the training program and disbanded. A task force was then put into place in fall 2017 and given specific charges to accomplish within the realm of service improvements for the university.

DeCenzo shared the following vision about CCU's service initiative: "We must together build a strong, university-wide culture of exceptional service where everyone can 'Feel the Teal.' By focusing on undergraduate and graduate academic excellence and good academic customer service, we will see an increase in student willingness to learn and engage not only in their studies, but also in experiential learning and leadership activities. Good customer service will better enable us to offer a quality product – education."

Training or Professional Development Program

All Coastal Carolina University employees are strongly encouraged to participate in Feel the Teal® trainings. There is an established certificate program that includes eight training modules focused on various service topics: the service basics, attitude, civility on campus, history and traditions, assisting with difficult situations, personal accountability, and a SWOT (strengths, weaknesses, opportunities and threats) workshop. The final training module is a celebration and includes a certificate, lunch, and a picture with President DeCenzo handing them their certificates of accomplishment.

Coastal Carolina University piloted its first training with University Recreation using a training module called "CCU Service Basics" on August 15, 2012. This training was created to identify a brand of service that needed to happen in every department. It helped to prepare staff with the needed service skills for the opening of the HTC Student Convocation and Recreation Center and continues to be used in hiring and training within the University Recreation operations.

University Recreation student-employees who completed the customer service training program emphatically stressed that the transference of skills for the real world was extremely beneficial with their career exploration, especially with interviews. Customer service was something they could reference in an interview or apply during an internship, and this added skill provided them with a career edge. "This training not only helped me with my job on campus, but it will help me with my future jobs," one student-employee said in a training evaluation.

The Service Mindset is the follow-up training program offered to employees so they can continue to grow the service mindset and stay engaged. These trainings were created from feedback gathered at the end of the Feel the Teal® training program, and the series includes a campus tour to learn more about the history and traditions, service book discussions, Servicescape audit training workshops, and more.

Recognition Method

Coastal Carolina University currently has several ways to recognize service providers for their excellence. Chauncey's Champions is a recognition effort that gives employees opportunities to celebrate others for their service excellence at CCU. It recognizes employees who go above and beyond in providing service to an internal or external customer. Areas of recognition are based on values specified in the SERVQUAL model of service quality:

- **Reliability:** Provides dependable and honest service by going above and beyond for customers.

- **Responsiveness:** Offers prompt and efficient service that creates a fast and friendly experience.

- **Assurance:** Acts knowledgably to listen and creatively solve problems for others.

- **Empathy:** Demonstrates excellent care and understanding.

- **Tangibles:** Displays, improves, and serves others through professional tangibles in all settings.

DeCenzo strongly encourages all employees, supervisors, and/or others in the employee's administrative channel to use this program when they hear about or observe exceptional customer service interactions. It is his hope that Chauncey's Champions will serve as a visible reminder to the community of the service priority in place. "Feel the Teal® is a successful initiative because of the effort and vision of our employees. Chauncey's Champions is a unique and spontaneous way that we can all unite as members of Teal Nation in an effort to celebrate our successes," said DeCenzo.

Service Excellence Champions are employees who have been recognized by a customer, internal or external for their service. These are submitted online via a web form where the customer can explain the exceptional service. Employees who receive the recognition are highlighted on the university website and in a monthly newsletter sent to all of the university community.

Presidential Thank Yous are a way that the president of the University publicly recognizes employees for their exceptional service. Employees and all other customers may submit an individual to the Feel the Teal® team to be recognized. A surprise recognition time is coordinated with the selected employee's supervisor. President DeCenzo then visits the employee while they are working to recognize them with a bouquet of balloons and a plaque.

A Presidential Thank You from Dr. DeCenzo.

Evaluation and Accountability

Coastal Carolina University's employment performance management system's evaluation program includes 10% allocation related to customer service skills. Supervisors are encouraged to share service successes so they can be celebrated through the Feel the Teal® office.

Measurement Tied to Retention

At Coastal Carolina University, measurement tied to retention is a constant conversation, and CCU is hoping to include more universities in this ongoing discussion. CCU recently started the Association for Service Excellence in Higher Education to advance, strengthen, and promote service excellence within higher education through ongoing collaboration, research, and leadership. The group will be a network of diverse professionals who support the concept of customer service within higher education and are dedicated to the collaboration of ideas, best practices, customer retention, and engagement.

For more information about the Feel the Teal® service excellence initiative at Coastal Carolina University, check out: https://www.coastal.edu/feeltheteal.

University System of Georgia

Public University System
Approximately 30 USG institutions

Georgia created statewide efforts to provide better customer service to its students through former Governor Sonny Perdue's "Customer Service Improvement

Initiative" in 2006. "Each Georgia citizen who walks through our door for a government service is an opportunity," said Perdue. "It is my intention that Georgia government employees will take advantage of those opportunities, showing citizens that we respect and value their time."

Chancellor Davis of the University System of Georgia (USG) ruled that all USG campuses had to implement customer service improvement programs. In February of 2013, Chancellor Huckaby requested an evolution of the Customer Service Program. As a result of that charge, the USG Service Excellence Program (SEP) was established to provide the platform for a higher level of coordination of performance-based partnerships resulting in enhanced student experiences and success. This program provided more alignment with USG's goals to enhance retention, progression, and graduation rates.

USG's service values are: *respectful, accessible, supportive, responsive, and informed.* These service values are supported through a clear mission, goal, and focus statements (see below).

- **Mission:** "The USG Service Excellence program promotes initiatives that unite the System in service and quality. These initiatives focus on the effective and efficient use of resources to support the success of our students, faculty, staff, and communities."

- **Goal:** "Increase the attention we give to improving services that support educational attainment, provide accountability, improve performance, and demonstrate value."

- **Focus Statements:** "1) We will develop projects that support student success by removing administrative obstacles. 2) We will remove other barriers that discourage enrollment or impede college completion. 3) We will focus on positively impacting our students' total education experience, community partnership, and faculty and staff engagement."

Leadership or Advisory Group

There is a strong leadership presence throughout the initiative. The president at each University System of Georgia (USG) campus is responsible for leading two service excellence projects during the fiscal year. One project should increase service to students. The other project should increase effectiveness and efficiency. At least one of the projects should contain an academic component. These projects contribute to service and process improvement results throughout the University System of Georgia (e.g., Kennesaw State University's 2017 project, "Human Resources Customer Service Survey and Improvements").

Training or Professional Development Program

In order to transfer the skills needed to ensure that interactions with Georgia State agencies became "faster, friendlier and easier," a training program was designed and developed. "Art of Exceptional Customer Service" was provided for more than 400 employees by the year 2013. Training continues to be supported; the 2015-2016 strategic plan also included a comprehensive customer service training program.

Recognition Method

The University System of Georgia recognizes and rewards employees for delivering consistently high levels of

performance while accomplishing normal job responsibilities as it relates to service for the previous year with the
Chancellor's Annual Service Excellence Awards. This is a
chance to highlight and celebrate the service projects and
their results for the good of the entire USG. Nominations
are accepted year-round, and employees are strongly
encouraged to submit nominations for:

- Outstanding individual

- Outstanding team

- Outstanding leader (administrator level)

- Outstanding process improvements

- Outstanding front desk support excellence award

- Outstanding institution

- Outstanding president

- Service excellence ambassador of the year

That is *eight* awards for service excellence!

For more information about the University System of
Georgia's service excellence program, check:

http://www.usg.edu/service_excellence/

Pace University

New York, New York
Private institution
8,914 undergraduate students

Pace University offers more than 100 undergraduate programs and 249 graduate programs, 29 of which are doctoral. Graduate program areas include health, arts, science, business, education, law, and technology. Pace University employees 1,213 staff and 510 full-time faculty.

The *I Make It Happen* customer service initiative at Pace University grew out of a commitment to creating and sustaining a caring, responsive, and student-centric service culture among staff that positively impacts the daily lives of students. Improving the overall student experience at Pace bolsters student satisfaction, retention, and graduation rates.

Leadership or Advisory Group

From the beginning, this initiative garnered strong support and excitement from the highest levels of the university's academics and executive team. Pace formed an executive steering committee headed by the vice president of enrollment and placement, as well as multiple subcommittees consisting of participants from all levels of management whose purpose is to maintain the momentum of this initiative and develop plans for ongoing service improvements and measurements for success.

Training or Professional Development Program

The most important factor in the success of Pace University's *I Make It Happen* service initiative is providing staff with the ongoing development to support and sustain the five Pace Service Values and Standards—Accessible, Respectful, Professional, Accountable, and Proactive. Using Coastal Carolina University's Feel the Teal® Service Excellence Initiative as a model, Pace University designed a training curriculum to support the *I Make It Happen* service initiative that includes four distinct modules: Pace Service Standards; Communication with Service; The Pace Service Mindset; and History of Pace.

For the initial phase of this initiative, Pace University selected the most critical student-facing departments to participate in the training and follow-up activities in order to measure success. The Organizational Learning & Development Department within the Human Resources Department at Pace University worked closely with Eileen Soisson, executive director of Training, Development and Service Excellence at Coastal Carolina University, to develop the curriculum. The first two modules were introduced in the spring of 2017. Beginning in fall 2017, all four modules will be offered monthly on both the Westchester and New York campuses. Individuals completing the training will be recognized after completion of each module and, more formally, at a university-wide event once they complete the entire curriculum.

The training model includes the identification of Pace Service Ambassadors from each school/college and division who exemplify the five Pace Service Values. They will serve as champions of the *I Make It Happen* service initiative, as subject matter experts for customized training content, and as trainers for the training curriculum. After completion of a train the trainer workshop conducted by Human Resources, the Pace Service Ambassadors will rotate as trainers for the *I Make It Happen* training.

Susan Donahue, Director of Organizational Learning and Development, believes that a thoughtful, Pace-specific training curriculum which builds the skills, knowledge, and behavior required to incorporate Pace Service Values and Standards into day-to-day interactions will help guide staff to embrace service excellence to all Pace customers.

Recognition Method

Pace University has created a formal recognition program, YES (Your Excellence Shows) *I Make It Happen*, which provides recognition to Pace staff and student workers for exhibiting behavior that embodies the five Pace Service Values.

- Individuals are recognized as they complete each module.

- Formal recognition at a universitywide event once individuals complete the entire curriculum

- Formal recognition through YES (Your Excellence Shows)

For more information about Pace University's *I Make it Happen* service program, check:

https://www.pace.edu/mypace/i-make-it-happen?mpc=fs.

Rollins College

Winter Park, Florida
Private institution
2,642 undergraduate students

Rollins College offers 34 undergraduate majors and nine graduate programs in education, behavior analysis, public health services, human resources, liberal studies, the MBA, and the EDBA. There are currently 235 full-time faculty and 507 staff working at Rollins College.

In 2009, a rebranding initiative looked to consolidate the university's brand image. That began with the overhaul of the college's website. From there, questions arose about how the institution would be able to deliver the promises of the brand. A customer service approach then became more strategic, and a plan was put in place to address common service issues such as the handoff, where a student is dropped during a service exchange or interaction.

Rollins College worked with *Unleashing Excellence* author and consultant Teri Yanovitch to create and apply the necessary service strategy to their academic setting. Yanovitch and the Rollins leadership group worked to identify the key service standards that defines service excellence at Rollins College (see below).

Rollins College Service Standards

Responsive:

- Innovative, resourceful, and timely

- Approachable and open-minded

- Solution-oriented

- Personalized and caring

- Balancing individual and institutional needs

Respectful:

- Friendly, courteous, and considerate

- Exhibiting care and compassion when serving others

- Valuing different ideas and perspectives

- Treating others with dignity

Collaborative:

- Effective at communicating within and outside of our immediate work groups

- Working together to accomplish departmental and institutional goals

- Demonstrating teamwork across boundaries

- Supporting others in what they do

- Keeping our eye on the big picture

Competent:

- Thorough knowledge of job and institutional mission

- Effective, efficient, and reliable performance

- Proficient in meeting student and customer needs

- Ability to align our efforts with departmental and institutional goals

- Ongoing commitment to excellence, innovation, and continuous improvement

Leadership or Advisory Group

"Service excellence will continue to play an important role in our overall success; to this end, the College has a service philosophy and service standards to help delineate what we consider important as we engage in our work and with each other, as colleagues, to deliver a seamless service experience to our students and customers," said current university president Grant Cornwell about the value of service excellence at Rollins College.

There is a strong leadership commitment to this initiative, and that was a huge difference maker at the beginning of the program according to Matt Hawks, Human Resources Director. Hawks shared that the service initiative has been one of the most successful and sustainable projects during his 20 years at Rollins, and much of that credit goes to the leadership and the service excellence team (and sub-teams).

The Rollins Service Excellence Team is a cross-functional management team made up of representatives from throughout the institution; currently there are 13 members. This group is given full authority to make and implement decisions as they relate to the service issues. Many positive changes have come forth because of this empowerment and leadership structure.

Sub-teams then support the service excellence team through these specific areas of responsibility and focus:

- Recognition and Events Sub-Team

- Orientation, Recruitment, and Training Sub-Team

- Service Obstacle System Sub-Team

- Communication Sub-Team

- Measurement and Accountability Sub-Team

Sub-teams are comprised of department heads, chairs, and their service representatives. Participants are selected based on their experience, passion, or interest in the service area, and on the best fit for the sub-team. Positions are rotating and inclusive to all areas so there is representation across the colleges.

Training or Professional Development Program

Rollins introduces its new employees to their culture and service philosophy during their new employee orientation. Thirty minutes is allotted to address customer service and the concept of servant leadership. Employees participate in a two- to three-hour introduction to service excellence where they learn tips and strategies for delivering great service at Rollins. Supervisory and leadership training is also offered to support customer service and what that means at Rollins.

Rollins College offers training for its employees to support their service mission. STARSS (Striving to Achieve Rollins Service Standards) is a continuous series of speakers, discussion forums, workshops, books clubs, video resources, and events. Rollins encourages employees to attend at least one of the STARSS events every year.

Recognition Method

Rollins College has a variety of recognition methods to reward employees for going above and beyond when interacting with a customer.

The Wall of WOW is an ever-growing collection of accolades from faculty, staff, and students designed to spotlight spontaneous service moments, random acts of kindness, and unexpected gestures that exude the service philosophy. Someone can fill out an online form to send a WOW message (Service Excellence Electronic Recognition Card) to an employee who has exhibited service excellence. That employee then receives a big WOW from representatives of the university, including members of the executive committee and/or the university mascot Tommy Tar. This Traveling Tommy circulates among employees who demonstrate service excellence. Someone can also publicly recognize a colleague on the Wall of Acknowledgment.

You've provided a WOW service experience!

The Service Excellence Departmental Award is an annual award that is presented to the team that has been consistent in using the four service standards to assist others. This involves a trophy and a plaque at the Awards Celebration. The trophy is rotated each year, but the plaque is kept. Department members also receive gift cards to the Rollins College Bookstore.

In 2016, Rollins implemented a gold coin recognition system in honor of the 12th university president, Thaddeus "Thad" Seymour, who used to walk around campus with silver dollars in his pocket. He was known to go out of his way to award someone with a silver coin if he heard of exemplary efforts made on behalf of a service solution. The gold coins have the service logo on them, and the goal is to pass them on once someone receives one and make it an ongoing way to recognize outstanding employees. What a creative way to keep history and traditions alive on a campus and also recognize people!

The Service Excellence Award recognizes a department or team that consistently demonstrates a high degree of excellence in teamwork and collaboration with other groups/departments, and that has proven its willingness to assist others in the Rollins College community responsively, respectfully, collaboratively, and competently. The Annual Service Excellence Awards Banquet is traditionally held the Friday before Memorial Day. More than 400 employees attend in great anticipation of the president's announcement of the winning department.

Evaluation and Accountability

Rollins addresses evaluation and accountability through the Measurement and Accountability Sub-team, the Service Obstacle System, and continuous research and data collection. The Service Obstacle System allows members of the campus community to point out obstacles to service excellence. It is an "online problem resolution system." Rollins created an internal survey that helps address and monitor service levels and establishes a score of 5 as the threshold so all areas could compare and contrast university-wide. This college truly wants to get better, and this is adopted into the ethos of the school.

The program at Rollins is a great example and model for other higher educational institutions to follow. This college truly embraces its service philosophy: "Together, we inspire purposeful lives through distinctive, engaged learning and exceptional service."

For more information about Rollins College's Service Excellence initiative, visit:

http://www.rollins.edu/service-excellence

Conclusion

For those in higher education, it is not a matter of **whether** they will serve their customers, but **how** they will serve their customers as a competitive advantage. Kotler and Fox state, "the best organization in the world will be ineffective if the focus on 'customers' is lost." This applies to higher education, and the sooner universities and colleges start to have this conversation, the better.

Coastal Carolina University surveyed more than 100 institutions about customer service programs, and 46% of the respondents said their institution was going to implement a customer service program of some sort within the next year. It is expected that more customer service programs are going to emerge from institutions of higher education. Newer programs will be looking to the early adopters for guidance and best practices. Schools with the necessary leadership, a customer service training program, a recognition program, and a method of evaluation and measurement will be steps ahead of the rest. The institutional profiles in this chapter provide examples of institutions that are doing this and doing it well. It is our challenge to you to use this information as a resource and a set of examples for your customer service program in higher education.

Visit these institutions; study how they are building customer service excellence and momentum. Take ideas back to inform critical conversations on your own campus.

GET CERTIFIED AS A CUSTOMER SERVICE PRO

Become a customer service expert by attending one of Academic Impressions' certification trainings. These events provide in-depth instruction with top customer service experts in higher education, and allow plenty of time for role-playing and practicing the core skills of good customer service. The conference culminates in a final, written exam, and you will receive a certificate of completion for your time spent and knowledge gained at this event. Show that your campus is a leader in customer service: get your entire front-line staff certified! We also provide on-campus certification workshops.

Interested? Contact Amit Mrig, President, Academic Impressions:

amit@academicimpressions.com

WORKS CITED

Albrecht, Karl, and Ron Zemke. *Service America! Doing Business in the New Economy.* Dow Jones-Irwin, 1985.

Bacal, Robert. *Perfect Phrases for Customer Service.* McGraw-Hill Education, 2010.

Blanchard, Ken, and Sheldon Bowles. *Raving Fans: A Revolutionary Approach to Customer Service.* William Morrow and Company, 1993.

Blanchard, Ken, and Spencer Johnson. *The One Minute Manager.* Berkley Trade, 1986.

Borowski, Craig. "What Customers Think About Call Center Scripts: 2014-2018." Hello Operator. 2014. Retrieved from: http://hello-operator.softwareadvice.com/what-customers-think-call-center-script-0514/

Boyd, Ricky. "Customer Service in Higher Education: Finding a Middle Ground." *The Mentor.* Penn State Division of Undergraduate Studies. 18 June 2012. Retrieved from: http://dus.psu.edu/mentor/2012/06/customer-service-in-higher-education/

Carnegie, Dale. *How to Win Friends and Influence People.* Simon & Schuster, 2010. Originally published 1936 (revised 1981).

Carlzon, Jan. *Moments of Truth.* Harper Business, 1989.

Cloud, Henry. *9 Things You Simply Must Do to Succeed in Love and Life.* Integrity Publishers, 2004.

Collins, Jim. *Good to Great: Why Some Companies Make the Leap…And Others Don't.* Harper Business, 2011.

Drahota, Amy, et al. "The vocal communication of different kinds of smile." *Speech Communication*, vol. 50, no. 4, 04/08, pp. 278-287.

"Effective Call Center Scripts." Salesforce Hub. Retrieved from: https://www.salesforce.com/hub/service/guide-to-effective-call-center-script/

Emery, Charles, et al. "Customers vs. products: Adopting an effective approach to business students." *Quality Assurance in Education,* vol. 9, no. 2, 2001, pp. 110–115. Retrieved from: http://www.bus.lsu.edu/accounting/faculty/lcrumbley/customersVSproducts.htm

Ewers, Jr., James B. "Using good customer service in higher education marketplace." *Diverse Issues in Higher Education,* 2 April 2010.

Fusch, Daniel. "Diagnosing the Barriers to Improving Customer Service." *Academic Impressions.* 12 December 2012. Retrieved from: https://www.academicimpressions.com/diagnosing-the-barriers-to-improving-customer-service-2/

Hampson, K. "Customer Service and/or Academic Standards." *Higher Ed Management,* 16 October 2011.

Kouzes, James M. & Barry Z. Posner. *The Leadership Challenge: How to Make Extraordinary Things Happen in Organizations.* Jossey-Bass, 2008.

Lehman, John. "Servicescape Audit." Co-developed with Academic Impressions and included in the conference

proceedings for Academic Impressions' annual
Customer Service training and certification.

Leidner, R. *Fast Food, Fast Talk: Service Work and the
Routinization of Everyday Life.* University of California
Press, 1993.

"New Research Shows Consumers Are Savvy to Scripted
Service Encounters." David Eccles School of Business
and Method Communications. *Business Wire*, 10 July
2012. Retrieved from:
https://www.businesswire.com/news/home/20120710
005753/en

Peters, Thomas, and Robert H. Waterman. *In Search of
Excellence.* Harper & Row, 1982.

Raisman, Neal. "Customer Service: The Key to
Enrollment and Retention Success." *Great Service
Matters,* Spring 2006. Retrieved from:
http://www.greatservicematters.com/gsm/media/pdf/
Customer_Service-
Keys_to_Enrollment_and_Retention.pdf

Raisman, Neal. *Embrace the Oxymoron: Customer Service in
Higher Education.* LRP Publications, 2002.

Sandborn, Mark. *The Fred Factor: How Passion in Your Work
and Life Can Turn the Ordinary into the Extraordinary.*
Currency, 2004.

Sandborn, Mark. *Fred 2.0: New Ideas on How to Keep
Delivering Extraordinary Results.* Tyndale House
Publishers, Inc., 2013.

Sanders, Betsy. *Fabled Service: Ordinary Acts, Extraordinary
Outcomes.* Jossey-Bass Publishers, 1995.

Stewart, D. M. "Piecing Together Service Quality: A Framework for Robust Service." *Production and Operations Management*, 2003.

Victorino, Liana, et al. "Can Customers Detect Script Usage in Service Encounters? An Experimental Video Analysis." *Journal of Service Research*, vol. 15, no. 4, 2012, pp. 390-400.

Service Examples

Coastal Carolina University's Feel the Teal® service excellence initiative: https://www.coastal.edu/feeltheteal

Pace University's I Make it Happen program: https://www.pace.edu/mypace/i-make-it-happen?mpc=fs

Rollins College's Service Excellence initiative: http://www.rollins.edu/service-excellence

University System of Georgia's service excellence program: http://www.usg.edu/service_excellence/

University of Central Michigan's service excellence program: https://www.cmich.edu/fas/hr/serviceexcellence/Pages/default.aspx.

———————————

Ritz-Carlton: http://www.ritzcarlton.com/en/about

Starbucks: https://www.starbucks.com/

Tom's Shoes: http://www.toms.com/

Walt Disney Company: https://www.thewaltdisneycompany.com/about/

Zappo: https://www.zappos.com/

ABOUT THE AUTHORS

Dr. Heath Boice-Pardee

Dr. Boice-Pardee has worked as an administrator in higher education for twenty-five years in a variety of administrative and teaching roles. Heath is currently the Associate Vice President for Student Affairs, and has served as Interim Senior Vice President for Student Affairs, at Rochester Institute of Technology (RIT). Additionally, he is a member of the faculty in the College of Applied Science and Technology at RIT and has developed a higher education administration Master's concentration focusing on service leadership, customer service, and the student experience. This is a one of a kind program in the world.

Additionally, Heath holds an appointment as an associate faculty member with the School for Advanced Studies at the University of Phoenix and was chosen as one of three faculty members to serve on an academic program council to develop a PhD in higher education program. In 2016, Heath was awarded a prestigious research fellowship from the Center for Leadership Studies and Educational Research on the topic: Identifying Value in Higher Education: A Practitioner's Perspective.

In 2018, Heath was elected the first Secretary of the Association of Service Excellence in Higher Education for its inaugural year.

Dr. Emily Richardson

Dr. Emily Richardson has been responsible for the adult learning populations in both online and seated modalities at the undergraduate and graduate levels since 2002, at three different universities. Currently, she holds the position of Director of the Hayworth Center for Online Learning at Queens University. Prior to this position, she was the associate vice president for Boundless Learning at Stetson University for two years. She began her education career at Widener University where she spent twenty-one years, initially teaching in the School of Hospitality Management. She also served as dean of the University College, a home for non-traditional students, prior to her departure.

Emily started her career in the hotel management industry, where she spent time in multiple positions throughout the United States and worked for companies such as Hyatt Hotels, Harvey House Hotels, and RockResorts. Her emphasis during most of her hospitality career was on training for customer service employees.

Since 2002, Emily has been a member of the University Professional and Continuing Education Association, has served on the board, as regional and cabinet chair, and currently is working on the network for small and specialized institutions.

Ms. Eileen Soisson

Eileen Soisson is currently the Executive Director of Training, Development and Service Excellence at Coastal Carolina University in Conway, SC. Since July 2011, Eileen Soisson has been leading CCU's service excellence initiative, Feel the Teal®, created to enhance the university's culture and become more service-oriented and focused on student success. Soisson designed the service excellence program's initial eight training modules, oversaw the implementation of the Service Mindset series, and oversees all operations within the initiative. She teaches university employees and others how to deliver better service within higher education. Soisson also oversees the Feel the Teal® Task Force at Coastal Carolina University and will be leading the Association for Service Excellence in Higher Education efforts to advance, strengthen and promote service excellence within higher education through ongoing collaboration, research, and leadership.

Eileen began her career in the hospitality industry and worked with the American Hospitality Academy for more than 10 years before starting her own business, The Meeting Institute, in 2004, which provides various training and development programs in the areas of leadership and customer service within the private sector. Her clients have included the U.S. Army, Audi of America, Metro Parks Tacoma, The Fountains Resort, the Myrtle Beach Area Chamber of Commerce Leadership Grand Strand Program, National Recreation Parks Association, and others.

In 2018, Eileen was elected the first president of the Association of Service Excellence in Higher Education, a new professional organization she has been instrumental in starting.

ACKNOWLEDGMENTS

The authors would like to thank the industries who offer countless ideas to improving customer service and the colleges and universities who are paving the way to enhance service excellence on-campus.

We would also like to thank the staff at Academic Impressions for championing this project and for being excellent partners.

47794656R00116

Made in the USA
Middletown, DE
10 June 2019